Twin Awakenings

Twin Awakenings

Raja and Santia

BALBOA.
PRESS

A DIVISION OF HAY HOUSE

ISBN: 978-1-4525-5434-1 (sc)
ISBN: 978-1-4525-5435-8 (hc)
ISBN: 978-1-4525-5436-5 (e)

Library of Congress Control Number: 2012910960

Balboa Press books may be ordered through booksellers or by contacting:

Balboa Press
A Division of Hay House
1663 Liberty Drive
Bloomington, IN 47403
www.balboapress.com
1-(877) 407-4847

Because of the dynamic nature of the Internet, any web addresses or links contained in this book may have changed since publication and may no longer be valid. The views expressed in this work are solely those of the author and do not necessarily reflect the views of the publisher, and the publisher hereby disclaims any responsibility for them.

The author of this book does not dispense medical advice or prescribe the use of any technique as a form of treatment for physical, emotional, or medical problems without the advice of a physician, either directly or indirectly. The intent of the author is only to offer information of a general nature to help you in your quest for emotional and spiritual well-being. In the event you use any of the information in this book for yourself, which is your constitutional right, the author and the publisher assume no responsibility for your actions.

Any people depicted in stock imagery provided by Thinkstock are models, and such images are being used for illustrative purposes only.
Certain stock imagery © Thinkstock.

Printed in the United States of America

Balboa Press rev. date: 6/22/2012

Dedicated to:
Abriel

It all started one day as I sat by the water's edge. I was waiting for something, hoping for something or rather someone.

My heart was longing, like I was missing the other half of my soul!

I was desperate to find her, but first I had to go deep within, to heal my spirit and to remember who I am.....

Contents

Chapter 1
Beginning to Love Me

My heart is open wide
As I learn to love myself.
Playfully I communicate
Openly speaking my truth
Dancing on the ground
To the beat of my heart.

* * *

There I was again, behind the wheel of my old pick-up truck, mindlessly driving down the narrow, windy stretch of mountainous road that I'd driven for years. No real destination. No time constraints, just me and the road, watching the trees pass outside my window.

I was lost in thought, day dreaming, when I saw a deer in the road about 100 yards in front of me. Suddenly I snapped out of it and quickly hit the brakes, screeching to a halt about a foot away from impact.

The deer didn't budge. It stood, calmly staring into my eyes as if it were reading me, mind and soul. After I caught my breath, I watched it watching me. I gazed back into its large brown eyes. A minute passed, maybe thirty. I was entranced by the presence of the deer. Slowly it nodded its head down and gracefully walked toward the trees on the opposite side of the road. Its eyes once again came in contact with mine. I waited until I could no longer see it moving through the forest, then drove away.

* * *

The rest of my drive home I was quiet, contemplating. My day's experience had rustled me at the core. Nearly 6:30pm when I pulled into my driveway. The sun was just setting in the sky.

I journeyed up to my special spot on the hill to lie down under the big oak tree. I meditated on the sunset, letting go of my day. Hazy pinks and oranges, mixed with blue, lavender and gold filled the evening sky. The air was warm and pleasing. I felt a great sense of peace through my whole body, my whole being.

A gentle sigh passed from my lips.

The once vibrant colors above me, now dark and blue highlighted by the moon. The stars began to peek out and twinkle throughout the sky. Slowly, I drifted into dreams. The same dream in fact, that I've had for the past two weeks.

There was this large crystalline sphere filled with bright, swirling energy and I was somehow inside it. I was certain a download with instructions for my stay on Earth was happening to me.

Information about my purpose for the journey, who I would encounter and the type of work I would engage in. There was this deep, clear knowing within me. I then tuned into a presence near me. It moved closer and all I could make out was a wispy, whitish energy body. It wrapped around me like a blanket, calming me, relaxing me at my core. I turned my head and our eyes met. The eyes like no other pulled me in. They were like two deep pools filled with light. I was sure they were speaking to me, knowing me, drawing me near and then…

I woke up.

I awoke to a cool breeze rustling the leaves above my head and headed back into the house. Cup of tea in hand, I sat next to the newly made fire. I wanted to relax, just sit and be but my thoughts were still on the dream. Why had I been in a sphere?

Where was I? And who was that being from my dream?

* * *

Two days later I met up with my best friend, Soni, for lunch. I was halfway through a sprout sandwich on rye, when I got the nerve to bring up my dream from the previous night. I explained that it was my recurring dream, except this time I couldn't tell myself apart from the other being. We seemed to merge together in the energy ball.

This time when I woke I was literally covered in beads of sweat and breathing heavily. Immediately upon waking, I grabbed a notepad and pen to write these words from my dream: "I am you."

It gave me chills even now speaking this to Soni and I felt shaky.

Soni listened attentively, foregoing the sandwich on his plate. I couldn't wait to hear what he had to say. He has this way of pulling deep truth and meaning out of nowhere and has an incredibly open mind.

At first he was quiet, then he said it was by far the strangest dream he'd ever heard. He also mentioned that he thought that my dream sounded like a kind of telepathic communication from outside of our usual planetary system. He further explained that my dream seemed to be showing how my path was unfolding, maybe even what was to come.

I sat back in my chair and thought about that. Something was unfolding.

Back at the house, I allowed my feelings to surface. Underneath my curiosity was fear, scared that I would somehow 'mess up' and destroy this beautiful gift. There was also sadness inside me. How long I had been waiting to find my partner. I was lonely, tears streamed my face.

I walked outside to sit on the grass, to feel my emotions, to give them space to breathe.

* * *

Just past sun down I ventured off to meet up with Soni and his partner Raji at a Transformational Fire Circle held on an uninhabited part of a local Indian reservation. I had just completed a meditation to ease my mind and to connect in deeper with my emotions. The word 'transformational' rang in my ears. I was ready for that.

Driving my little truck didn't seem right tonight, so I walked and felt the earth beneath my feet. It was about 30 minutes walking time giving me plenty of opportunity for perspective. I looked above me and saw the outline of the trees. Crickets were the only sound. I took a deep breath and exhaled.

My body relaxed feeling in tune with nature and her inhabitants.

As I approached the fire circle, I saw Soni and Raji talking with a man I did not recognize. Yet something told me, it was someone I needed to know.

Before I had the chance to introduce myself, the group was called together to form around the fire. Drums began in a slow rhythm as we were led into a meditative state by a tall man with long dark hair. His energy felt powerful, like a gentle warrior. I closed my eyes and allowed myself to be taken away to a sweet inward space. The energy inside me began to build and build. My inhibitions finally dropped away.

The once dull drums now felt as if they were pounding in my head. I could hear others laughing and crying, yelling and screaming. Feeling my own release, cries erupted from me and I let out a long, deep howl from my belly.

"I am ready!" I yelled out loud. Then more softly as if to myself: "I am ready."

* * *

I awoke on the dusty ground by last night's fire circle. My sleep had been filled with magical dreams and I felt a sense of renewal. The only one, besides me, that was awake was the man that Soni and Raji were talking to right before the circle began. He looked to be in a quiet state, sitting on a large flat rock, facing the upcoming sun. He heard my steps and without turning spoke to me: "You are waiting for her."

Stunned for a moment at his blunt statement, who was this man and why was he saying this to me. Then, a calm came over me, a rather sudden but peaceful calm that I've never felt before.

Without questioning why, I replied "Do you know who she is?"

He replied matter-of-factly "She is You."

* * *

My life had always seemed simple. I walked in unison with the Earth and her creatures, I have been living consciously, an aware being, believing in realities beyond what I see with my eyes. Yet, something was changing, something I wasn't aware of, or prepared for. My dreams started merging into my awake time. More and more frequently I am having experiences that cross realities and have me questioning space and time.

I was sitting under my favorite tree doing a Heart Opening Meditation. In my usual cross-legged position, sitting upright, balancing my energy with the earth and the sky. My focus was around my heart and heart chakra, in the center of my chest. I was opening up the energy in the chakra and clearing blocks preventing me from feeling fully alive. Just as I reached a place where all the blocks were cleared, a new energy came into my space. It wrapped around me and made my skin tickle and tingle, similar to having warm breath blown on your neck. Then, with my eyes open I saw a being in front of me. It was pleasant and looked like it was made from a cloud, a flowing kind of energy. Telepathically it requested that I follow it, so I got up and began walking. We were headed in the direction of the forest along side my home. When I looked down for a moment, I noticed that my feet appeared to be *above* the ground!

We came to a clearing about 500 yards into the forest where there was a small stream. The being stopped and requested that I step into the water—again telepathically. I did as it asked and immediately felt my body merge with the water and with the rocks, pebbles, sand and whatever else was in the stream that day! The feeling was so incredible and satisfying, like its energy was filling me to the point where I was not even hungry anymore, for anything.

When I returned home, I looked at the clock. It seemed like only minutes but I had been away for 5 hours. The funny part was I didn't even remember walking back.

* * *

Today was a day for clearing and connecting with the earth. It was heading into fall and I had much to do in my garden. Soni was on his way over to lend a hand. He used a quarter of the garden space for planting his own veggies.

He showed up just after lunch and we began pruning and preparing for winter. Usually a calm character, Soni suddenly stood up straight and went a bit pale in the face. He said that a voice was speaking to him, a voice he did not know.

My friend, though rather adventurous and mildly spiritually aware, hadn't experienced things like this before. Probably an untapped ability.

I asked him what the voice was saying. He began speaking for the voice: "I am Ashrial. I am here to bring a message of great importance." He paused.

"The time has come for awakening. You must prepare space for the truth. It is also time to open yourself to emotions of the heart. Journey to the mountains. Sit on the ground for three days. Bring nothing."

Soni stopped talking, he appeared to be back 'as usual' though a bit stunned. I looked over and smiled: "I guess we're going on a trip!"

His jaw dropped.

* * *

It was Friday evening when I drove over to Soni's place. We had opted for going on the weekend since Soni had a regular workweek. I was already on a guidance directed work leave, using some money I had put away.

I pulled into his driveway and he ran out the front door, waving a kiss goodbye to Raji. We headed down the road and up the mountain. The air was crisp and the forest looked rather pristine this evening. A bright, nearly full moon lit the sky. I remembered what Ashrial had said: Prepare space for the truth.

I said to myself: I'm ready for that.

We arrived at our parking spot, just off the road and we got out of the truck. Soni claiming to be an avid boy scout...still...ventured off to build a fire. I stood by a group of trees in the moonlight soaking in the lunar rays.

Within minutes he came back with kindling and large pieces of dry wood. We located some rocks in the area building a fire ring together. A few minutes of what looked like knocking some stones together and viola he started a fire.

(About a year ago I took a wilderness course. They always recommend bringing matches just in case. I did. Just in case.)

Once the fire was going strong, we pulled up a couple of large rocks next to our ring. Soni stared into the flame as if mesmerized. I wondered if he was thinking about what Ashrial said, too.

As if out of nowhere, he said: "I love her, you know."

I allowed him room to talk, space for the words to find their own way.

"She is everything to me," he said. "I've been holding back, not a lot, but enough. I'm ready to let go and spend the rest of my life with her."

I closed my eyes. His words felt peaceful to me.

"I'm ready to share this with her, to have a commitment ceremony... God I love her so much, brother."

"I Love Her!" he yelled and began to cry.

"Just let it go..." I whispered aloud.

I watched his energy over the next few minutes. First static red energy filled the air near him as he released pain, then a softer pinkish energy, almost fuzzy surrounded him.

He was brave. I was still holding on, maybe trying to be strong, unsure if she really existed. I went for a walk leaving room for him and making space for me, my truth.

If she is out there, I wanted to make sure there was room for her and me.

* * *

I headed down a small path, unsure where it led. The feeling and the words that Soni shared echoed within me. He loved her and he knew it, he was ready.

I wanted to be ready.

For years I've walked this life myself. I'm happy and all but I feel like something is missing. My heart feels empty in a way. It's like I have a key to a lock but I haven't found the door.

I'm afraid.

There I've said it, I am afraid!

Focusing on the feeling and allowing it to breathe, I began to let go.

I don't want to hold on anymore...I can't hold on!

I fell to my knees on the forest path, tears rolling, and then streaming my face. My body was shaking, every part of me shaking, vibrating and releasing my held pain.

"I want to make room for her!" I yelled. "I want to know who she is!"

Then softer: "Please come to me...I need you.... I...I can't do it anymore."

More tears, more sobs, more shaking.

I began yelling again.

"Take me if you need to, but don't leave me lonely!"

"Bring her to me!!" I yelled at the sky, as if there were someone there, holding me back.

I screamed, hollered, howled, sobbed, growled as loud as my voice would go.

"I'm ready to let it all go!!! I'm ready for truth!!!"

Tears continued and the rain came pouring down, helping release my pain. Thank you grandmother rain!

Sounds of thunder rumbled in the sky. I mimicked the sounds. Thank you thunder!

Lightning streaked the sky. Flashes of light came in unison with the roar from the thunder. Thank you lightning!

I was soaked in the rain from the sky and from my own pain.

Lying there on the ground, on the forest path, atop pine needles, rain soaked I surrendered.

* * *

When I wandered back over to our site, a smile poked its way out to see that Soni was standing there waiting for me with open arms and a toasty fire!

We hugged for a long while, feeling the softness that had come from all that releasing. Feeling grateful to be there together, sharing our experience.

Then we danced round the fire, chanting and laughing, feeling our emotions. The ground was damp when we lay down to sleep, but it felt rich.

We closed our eyes and drifted into dreams.

* * *

The morning sun warmed my face and I stretched myself awake. The air felt clean, the sky clear. I began my morning meditation, sitting on the ground, my eyes closed, breathing in the earth's energy, and feeling the beginning of a new day. Energy coursed through me and I felt alive again, renewed.

When I finally opened my eyes, I saw Soni sitting on the ground next to me, cross-legged, eyes closed and meditating!

I stood again and stretched once more, this one a long full body stretch to really wake me up. Soni and I telepathically agreed to go for a hike up the mountain. We started up a trail unknown to us, always an exciting experience for me taking the road not yet traveled. We walked in silence, a peaceful quiet that allowed me time for inner contemplation.

I said to myself, "I am ready for truth, ready for emotion, ready for love I would live for."

The top of my head started getting buzzy and light. A melty white energy surrounded me, giving me pleasant shivers. I had the feeling that we weren't alone. A being outside human form was near and drawing closer.

I felt something moist and tingly on my cheek, like a kiss. My skin became hot, I was flushed and breathing heavy. I looked around and could no longer see Soni. It appeared that I was now by a stream deeper in the woods. A small waterfall splashed down into a pool.

It seemed so inviting. I walked over to feel the temperature of the water. Mmmm, perfect! Seeing no one else around, I left my clothes hanging on the branch of a tree and climbed in.

The hot energy intensified, the shivers made my whole body shake. I sighed aloud. It felt like I was receiving a massage. Relaxation. Absolute relaxation. The white energy wrapped around, cradling me gently. I felt full.

I was complete.

* * *

I found myself sitting on a rock slab next to Soni at a mountain lookout spot. It was serene, with a slight breeze, surrounded by pine trees. In the distance there were more trees and several hills. Below was a valley looking lush and green. Blues and purples on the horizon. What a magnificent niche he found for us, such a place to rest and feel the mountain.

I wonder if he noticed that I was gone?

Dusk was upon us as we hopped down the hill to our site. When we arrived, Soni built another fire and sat on his rock. My mind drifted off, thinking about my earlier experience by the waterfall. The feeling stayed with me, the feeling that I am not alone anymore. She must be close, I thought. I wonder when we will meet?

With that thought, I sent a transmission to Soni that I was out for the night.

I lay my body down on a soft bed of pine needles to catch some dreams.

* * *

My dreams were fast and frantic. I was running to catch her, running to find out where she was going. There was no recollection of her upon waking.

The morning air was strange today. It had a lurking feeling not bad but slightly eerie. When I woke, Soni was already up and pacing.

This time speaking aloud he said, "I think something's about to happen."

Me too.

Just then the wind picked up. The leaves on the trees were whipping about, throwing pine needles and leaves around the area. My breathing was more rapid and goose bumps covered me, head to toe. My legs began shaking uncontrollably from the incoming energy.

Suddenly we were both inside a sphere of swirling light. I could still see the trees in the forest and my feet were on the ground, but this sphere surrounded us. The energy inside was like static, zapping above and around Soni and I.

The focus of my eyes shifted and I could now see the structure of a planetary system just in front of me. The planets were circling. I saw that they were about to align, all of them. There were probably 50. The static intensified and the planets whirled faster and faster. Then a flash of light, so bright I winced, almost having to turn away.

When I opened my eyes fully, I was amazed.

In front of me was one planet.

I said aloud: "She's coming!"

Chapter 2
We Two Are One

Back at home again...Soni and Raji were planning their commitment ceremony. They never looked happier. It made my heart warm to see them this way.

I on the other hand felt a bit deflated compared to all that high energy on our mountain trip. Thoughts were stirring in me. Wondering where she was now and how soon would I meet her face to face.

The fifteenth of next month was the ceremony and I hoped she'd be here by then.

I didn't want to go alone, not without her.

Then a week after our trip, things began picking up. My phone was ringing off the hook. People that I hadn't talked to in ages were calling, saying they were just thinking of me or some even said they followed their intuition to call.

Shortly, I'd been invited to three workshops—a relationship intensive, a heart-opening circle and a sweat lodge. There was also one invitation to play drums at a sacred earth music festival. I was blown away.

Spirit was guiding me toward something. That was for sure!

* * *

The weekend was here and so was the sacred earth music festival. I planned to meet up with my old friend, Elu, just before the festival. I drove over to the Indian reservation at about 5:30pm. Elu parked by the fence. I followed his lead and parked there as well.

It was good to see him again.

He smiled and walked toward me, arms open for an Elu Bear Hug.

God, I missed him.

I caught him up on my latest adventures...like the mountain trip, about my encounter with an energy presence and the message that my 'she' was coming soon.

He hugged me again with congratulations and asked if it was okay to give a blessing.

I agreed.

Elu lit his smudging stick and gave a blessing to protect me. He murmured some things in his native tongue while making rings around me. He marked me with ash from his stick. Then pressed his flat hand in the middle of my chest, pulled in closer and whispered: "And I bestow blessings to you Roo'kystana. May you come swiftly and safely into his waiting arms."

* * *

What!!!

"Who is Roo'kystana?" I asked, practically demanding.

"Come, let's go play our drums," Elu replied and began walking in the direction of the melodic thumping now filling the air.

Who is she? I wondered to myself. Was it her, the being that came to me on the mountain?

"Elu, please tell me," I said trying to catch up with him.

But that was that. Elu wasn't about to reveal this secret to me... yet. Hard as it was, I tried to put it aside. I tried to center my thoughts again.

Focus on my heart. Breathe deep.

We met up with the rest of the group. They were already drumming. Their hands vibrating with the rhythms. Some had tall drums, others had small hand held drums and a few were playing flutes.

As I hit my hands in different patterns on the top of my drum, I sung that name.

Roo'kystana, Roo'kystana, Roo'kystana, over and over in my mind. Silently I was making a connection to her, bridging over to our future. She was tapping her way into my life and my heart.

Roo'kystana, Roo'kystana. Another set of thumps on the drum.

Roo'kystana, Roo'kystana, Roo'kystana. Beating louder now, expressing more power.

"Roo'kystana, Roo'kystana," I started to say her name aloud, unaware that I was at first.

Chanting her name, others joined me: "Ay, ay, Roo'kystana, ay, Roo'kystana."

The sound of the drums, intertwined with the flutes echoed in the air. Sweat poured down my cheek.

As the song ended, Elu turned to me and said: "Roo'kystana. The other half of your flame, brother." A smile spread over his face. "Your soul will not be lonely anymore."

My eyes wet, I looked into his eyes and smiled, too.

Roo...the other half of my flame.

Chapter 3
The Dark Forest

There is a weight upon our life
A dead feeling inside
Spirit gave us a taste of magic
Of connecting deep and feeling alive
The weight lifted for a moment
To help us remember our true essence
Now it is up to us to lift off the weight
To find the gentle, solid place
To feel peaceful and whole

* * *

It was Monday morning and I called a good friend of mine, Madam Rieshel.

I couldn't wait!

She is coming, my Roo, I needed to know when or where. Or both. I was sure Madam Rieshel would have the answers for me.

She picked up on the first ring and said that she was waiting for me to call her.

Ah...of course.... she is psychic.

"Rieshel, I was told that she's coming and what her name is...it's Roo'kystana...I call her Roo for short.... and I need to know when and where we'll meet...oh and is there anything I should do before then.... you know cut my hair, wash my clothes..."

Madam Rieshel cut me off mid sentence: "Slow down."

She always did get right to the point.

"Now, we need to meet in person. Come by my place in 30 minutes. I'll see you then," she said hanging up the phone.

Her shop was 10 minutes from here, so I left immediately. I couldn't wait!

* * *

Madam Rieshel answered the door with a shout: "Come in!"

"I'm in the back," she said once I was inside.

She was already sitting down in her favorite chair with her colorful, eccentric scarves wrapped around her. A small bright red, orange, gold patterned scarf on her head, a large scarf of multi-colored stripes and squares covering her neck and shoulders.

I took a seat, then stood up again.

"Rieshel, I need to know when and...."

She cut me off again: "Sit."

I sat.

She focused and closed her eyes, drifting into some unknown to me realm of answers.

"You have a lot of bags," she said at last.

Bags? I said to myself.

"Yes, bags," she began as if answering my silent question. "You have many things to clean up within you before she can come."

"What do you mean?" I queried.

"Many unfinished lessons from many lives, dark unlooked at corners of your soul, parts of you separated from the whole."

"How long will that take?" I gulped.

"A month, maybe six...it could take years." She opened her eyes and stared at me.

I sat back in my chair, my face blank, my hopes crushed, sitting with what she had just said.

* * *

I'd been in bed for nearly a week when Soni stopped by. He called but I didn't pick up. He left a message but I didn't call back.

So he stopped by.

He was tossing pebbles at my window and saying, "Hey, brother, I know you're in there. It's not that bad, you'll get through it I promise."

I pulled the covers higher and buried my head.

Next thing I know, Soni is walking through my bedroom door!

Oh yeah, that's right I gave him my spare house key. Darn.

"Brother, come on get up, let's talk." He started to pull back the mass of blankets now covering me. "Is that a box of cookies?"

Darn again. He found my under the blanket stash.

I've been eating a vegan raw food diet for the past two years. He had to know this was bad.

"Come on, brother, please get up." He was now pulling on my arms, attempting physical force to move me. "Potato chip bags? Ice cream wrappers? Brother, we are gonna need some help here...phew!"

I hadn't seen him so flustered before. It must be bad.

* * *

"Okay, okay, I'll get up." There I said it, now he could stop trying to remove my arms!

Soni and I sat at the kitchen table and my story began like this: "Soni, I can't go on. I can't wait years to find her, to hold her. That is just too much. Many lives, dark corners of my soul... I can't do it. I mean what do they want from me? Next thing you know they'll say 'Oh don't worry everything is exactly as it should be.' I'm going back to bed. Wake me up when they come to take my truck." I started to get up.

"Sit down. No one's coming for your truck, don't worry, you couldn't pay someone enough..."

"Ah, Soni?" I mean come on, I might be down under but really.

"Sorry," he replied quietly. "Look, brother, you have a lot going for you, a lot to live for. Roo is waiting for you, Raji and I are expecting you at our commitment ceremony." He winked at me, then continued: "We'll get through it together, okay? One step at a time."

I sat back in my chair. Okay, one step at a time.

* * *

After showering, I contacted Annie, leader of the heart-opening circle. She said they meet three times a week, Monday, Wednesday and Friday so I signed up for tonight's circle.

Meanwhile, Soni had gone and come back, this time bringing a large brown trash bag. He began tossing cookies, chips, wrappers and whatever else he could find.

I stepped outside to sit under my favorite tree on the hill. Thoughts stirred in my mind. I knew it was worth it for me to get all my unfinished stuff together. I knew that she was worth it, my Roo.

I missed her.

I took a deep breath and closed my eyes, centering my energy in my chest. I am ready for this, I said to myself. I am ready for change.

* * *

When I arrived at Annie's, everyone was sitting on meditation cushions in a circle. Annie saw me and stood up to motion me over.

"Welcome," she said to the group.

"Today's circle has a special format," she continued. "We are going to listen while each person shares from their heart about why they are here or a recent heart opening experience."

"We'll start to my left and go clockwise. Is everybody ready?"

Nods from all in our circle.

"Okay, Sally, we are open for sharing," motioning to the woman to her left.

First Sally spoke about her husband who had passed away and how she opened her heart to keep living. Then James (aka Buddy) cried and told of his recent experiences with feeling like a failure, and then me.

"I've never been in love before," I began slowly.

"I didn't believe that there was a soul partner for me, in fact, I truly didn't feel deserving. I just felt empty inside...lonely." Tears welled up and I started to sob.

"And part of me felt like giving up, like dying." I couldn't hold back anymore, the tears flowed freely down my face, my body shaking.

A light rain fell outside the window. I paused before continuing.

"But today, I decided to change all that and say 'yes' to opening my heart."

It was funny, I hadn't even realized before that I felt undeserving.

When the circle ended, I walked over to Annie and gave her a big hug.

I think this was the best night of my life.

* * *

It was the weekend again and I felt great! Last night I opened my heart more and signed up for other heart opening circles. Soni's commitment ceremony was tomorrow. He and Raji planned to have their friend, Saki, unite their souls forever. I couldn't wait!

Things were looking up.

My day started with a long meditation, centering again in my heart. I sat there until peace radiated from me.

I thought about things for a while before getting up and going inside. Then I made up my mind, it was time to clean up the house.

I got out a ladder so that I could reach my storage area where all the boxes were kept. Within a few minutes the storage area was cleaned up, boxes that were full of things I didn't need anymore were set on the floor below. I hopped down and folded the ladder up.

Quicker than a fox, I picked up the boxes one by one and carried them outside to place on the bed of my truck.

Last box. I leaned down to pick it up and Wham! My back went out. I was bent over and couldn't get back up. All I could do was stand there crying from the pain.

* * *

After a while I heard a whistle and then: "Hey brother! I brought some carrot juice for you..." Soni walked in the front door and saw me leaning over the box.

"You okay, brother?" he asked.

I couldn't answer really, so I squeaked: "Help."

Soni brought me in to lie down on the floor in the living area. There was a nice soft rug there. Then he ran upstairs to grab a pillow.

"What happened?" he asked once he returned.

"I don't know," I said. "One minute I was flying around cleaning and picking up boxes, next thing I know I'm frozen in pain."

"Hey, maybe you should come over, we're going to a friend of ours next door to soak in the tub." He looked me over. "I think you could use some of that."

He started to walk toward the front door. Turning his head, he yelled back, "I'll pick you up around four! Take care, brother." With that, he was gone.

There I was lying on the floor, looking up at the carrot juice that I couldn't reach and wondering...

How did I get into this mess?

* * *

We were driving toward his friend's house, Soni and I, when he asked where the pain was.

I pointed at the mid to lower part of my back.

He put on one of the CD's that he made. It was a combination of Native American drumming and Eastern chanting put together with a techno feel. I allowed myself to melt into the music. My mind had been way too busy today.

When we arrived, he helped me out of the car.

"You know, my back has been hurting, too," he said rubbing his lower back. "I think I'm having sympathy pains."

Raji came out to meet us. She gave a kiss to Soni and then: "Hey what happened, brother? Soni said you lifted too many boxes. Why didn't you ask for help?"

"Yeah, you know I would have helped...why didn't you ask?" Soni said right away.

Then he looked a bit wounded and said toward Raji: "You know, my back started hurting, too."

Raji had Soni's arm around her shoulder on one side and me on the other helping both of us to limp inside.

What a sight.

* * *

Raji introduced me to their friend and mentioned that she does breath work.

"You know, brother, you really should have Solana show you how to breathe," Raji said to me.

Show me how to breathe? I wondered.

"I can tell you a bit more, if you like," said Solana. "Or if you're ready, I can show you how to use breath work to heal your back."

Huh? Breathing to heal my back? I just lifted too much didn't I?

Just then there was a pinching feeling in my lower back.

"Okay, let's try it," I said aloud.

First we all got in the tub to start the relaxation process. Then Solana showed how to focus my breath into a specific area, in this case my back.

"Now, close your eyes and picture your breath filling the area. Watch it fill up and then release as you exhale," she said.

Oooh, that does feel good...so freeing.

"Inhale, fill your back with love, exhale release your pain," Solana reminded me.

Something started shifting.

"I see someone, a man, carrying a heavy load, like a pack," I said aloud.

"Yes, keep going," she urged me.

"His heart is full of dark clouds and it's raining outside."

"Now, inhale..." Solana kept the flow of breath going.

"He is lonely. He doesn't remember it being another way, just alone."

It touched in to my emotions. I felt like crying.

Exhale.

"He is walking away from town, away from civilization with a heavy pack on his back."

Inhale.

"God, I don't want to be alone anymore!" I cried. "I don't want to be lonely, it hurts!"

Exhale.

I cried loud and hard, deep from within the pain in my back, deep from within my soul.

Gently, Solana said: "What wisdom does your back have for you?"

Inhale.

"It says to remember who I am. Remember why I am here. Remember what love is. And to remember how to open my heart."

Exhale.

"It says that I push myself too much, trying. Trying to be and do things because I don't feel worthy of love, don't feel worthy of being alive."

Inhale.

"It says I need to go slow, trust in my emotions and listen to my body."

Exhale.

I dunked my head under water, then popped back up to wipe my face and open my eyes.

"Thank you body for sharing with me such wisdom." I gave a peaceful smile to Solana.

I think I'm starting to remember who I am.

Chapter 4

Celebrations!

"Hey brother! It's our big day, you coming over, or what?" Soni asked over the phone.

"Yes, I'm coming. Of course I'm coming, I wouldn't miss it for the world," I replied.

I paused.

"Doesn't the ceremony begin in two hours Soni?"

"Yes, but come over now anyway!" Soni ordered playfully and hung up the phone, leaving me no other option.

Off to Soni's place.

When I arrived there were a dozen cars in front of the house, there was music playing (I could hear it from the street) and sounds of people laughing.

The front door was open and I walked inside. Soni jumped out from nowhere and started talking.

"Brother!" He hugged me hard and slapped my back. "Brother, I'm having a baby...we're having a baby! Oh my god I am soo happy!! I have never been this happy, this elated, in all my life!!!"

I hugged him back, but not as hard, not as happy. I mean I was happy for *him* but oh so sad for me. Today was their commitment ceremony and Roo was not with me.

Soni and Raji are starting a family and I'm still alone.

I tried to play it off like it didn't hit home painfully.

"Soni, I'm really glad, brother. You deserve all the gifts the world has to offer." I squeezed out a smile.

* * *

I made an excuse and took a walk outside.

My best friend is beginning a new life, a new family. How do I support him without ruining his big day?

I felt a pinch in my lower back again.

That's right, listen to my body and breathe. I stood next to a tree and closed my eyes to meditate, to listen to my back and breathe life back into it.

Back what are you saying? What is the message you have for me?

Message: Don't hide how you feel, share it, let it out, be real and breathe.

I walked back to Soni's and pulled him aside to talk. I shared with him about my pain: "I am missing her, brother. You and Raji embarking on a new adventure together, reminds me that I am still alone. I hurt inside wondering how far I still need to go."

Soni reached his hand out to touch my shoulder.

"My brother, I'm sorry it hurts so much. Thank you for sharing your pain with me, for telling me your truth." Soni gave me a warm hug.

I think he even dropped a tear.

Chapter 5

Bringing Me Home

Deep within me
Is the truth of who I am
It is hiding
In the shadows of my mind
Inside my heart
Lies the answer, the key
I am learning
To unfold and embrace me
I am learning what love is

* * *

Again my dreams were intense. Last night I dreamt of Roo in a pale pink dress running barefoot on a forest path, long hair flowing behind her. I tried to catch up to her. I called her name over and over. Then I fell into a rabbit hole and woke up.

I called Elu and asked him what this dream meant. He was great at interpreting things.

Elu said that I was running from a fear and that I needed to go back to my past lives. He also said she represented part of me that I hadn't accepted yet and that it was time to call all of me home.

* * *

I felt lost in a way, unsure what step to take. I didn't feel capable of finding my parts and bringing them home.

I began questioning who I was, why these tasks were being asked of me. I didn't feel powerful or all knowing and I wasn't even sure who to ask for help.

I took a deep belly breath and focused inside of me. I said to myself, I am ready for answers, ready for truth, and ready for help.

Exhale.

Just then my phone rang. It was Marty an old friend of mine. He shared that last night he dreamt of me, for the first time in fifteen years. So he decided to call me today.

I shared my latest...about Roo and about my pile of unfinished work that needs to be completed before Roo can come to me.

We talked for over an hour.

Marty and I planned to meet up later today for lunch by the lake.

At one o'clock I pulled into the lake parking area and parked next to a tree. Marty wasn't there yet so I found us a nice place to sit and set up a blanket. I made a salad earlier and brought a container of fresh lemonade.

When Marty arrived we took a long walk. There were many paths around the lake. It was fun finding different birds and plants along the way.

Marty spoke about his life so openly. He had been married before, now divorced. They parted ways peacefully and remained good friends. Since that time, he started teaching Wake Up Spirit classes, a class devoted to bringing alive all parts of you and the divine being that you are.

My body twitched...it sounded like exactly what I needed.

* * *

The weekend was coming and I was going to Marty's two-day class. Ever since I signed up for the class, my body was beginning to wake up. There was energy zinging through me and I could now easily focus on my breath work.

The class was held about an hour and a half away from me. I enjoyed the time to myself to think and breathe. I drove slowly and listened to my body. If it wanted to stop, I pulled over. If it wanted water, I gave it water. If it wanted to cry, I cried.

I arrived a bit early and had a chance to meet with Marty and his partner, Jon. It turns out that Marty met Jon when he attended a Wake Up Spirit class and now they are teaching it together.

There was a circle of chairs, about fifty of them and slowly the room filled with people talking and moving about to find a seat.

I was a bit intimidated. What if I wasn't ready for this?

Jon began the class with a short meditation. I closed my eyes and listened to his words:

"Wake up Spirit! Wake up gently,wake up strong. I ask of you: Spirit, Do you want to be Alive? Do you want to say yes to freedom? Freedom from pain, freedom from patterns?"

I could hear others saying yes softly. I said yes, too.

Jon continued: "Spirit let me hear you loud and strong. Let me hear you when you say yes to being Alive, yes to freedom and yes to bringing all of you home!"

My body jumped...those were the words I was looking for...yes to bringing all of me home.

I say YES.

* * *

In talking stick style, we each took a turn speaking when the stick was passed to us. As the talking stick went around the circle, people shared their experiences. Some times one person would have the stick for thirty minutes. Emotions flowed as they revisited experiences and brought healing to them.

Jon walked each person through finding love inside. He helped them untangle old beliefs they had made about themselves and how the world works.

Space was made for them to feel and open up. As long as they held the stick, the floor was theirs.

It was just after the break that the stick was handed to me. Jon coached me so that I could uncover some old wounds.

First he asked me to focus on the emotion that I was feeling.

"I feel sad and scared as well," I said aloud.

"That's good. Now, where in your body is that feeling? Go ahead and point to it," said Jon.

I pointed just below my heart.

"Okay, place your hand over this spot and breathe into it. Feel your hand move with your breath as you inhale and exhale," Jon said walking me through. "Once you feel your breath moving in it, allow any memories or images to come up. You can speak them aloud if you're comfortable with that."

I felt my breath and watched my hand move up and down with the flow of breath.

"I see something," I said.

"Okay, what position is your body within this memory?" Jon asked.

"I am standing," I replied.

"Now, step into the experience and let the feeling wash over you," said Jon.

As I stepped into this memory and let the experience wash over me, I noticed I was in a different body, living in a different country and time.

So this is what a past life is, I thought. It is a memory just like any other ones.

I started to wander in thought.

Jon helped me stay focused on the feeling. "The feeling is important. Let the understanding come afterward," he said.

"I see Roo, in this life we had found each other," I began. "The energy in me was very high. But not completely balanced."

"Please continue," said Jon.

"People around me seem to be drawn to my high energy. They have a similar imbalance though. These people are directing anger and fear toward me. They want to hurt me," I said breathing heavier, feeling scared.

"Step back a bit from this experience. Remember, you are safe here with us," Jon said slowing things down.

I stepped back from the intense energy and felt calm again.

I continued: "The people around me are confused and they hurt my body, I can't find Roo anymore. Now I see myself crossing over into the light. My spirit has left my body. Someone took my life." I sat back feeling more relaxed. "It's okay now, I feel peaceful."

Jon said to step out of the experience now, it was time to come back fully into my body.

I cried feeling the sorrow of losing Roo and myself.

Aloud I thanked this part for sharing the experience and welcomed it back home. The spot just below my heart felt softer and lighter.

Jon recommended another break for everyone. Just as I was about to leave, he called me over.

"Could I share some things with you?" he asked.

I turned around and replied: "Sure."

"You know, that was an amazing release you just experienced," Jon said slowly. "It would be good for you to take some time for yourself. It is important to have room for the full emotions to release."

I nodded in agreement. "I think I will go ahead and skip out on the rest of today's class." I thanked him and headed home to be with my feelings.

* * *

When I returned home, spirit called me to my secret spot down by the river.

I sat down by the river's edge, watching the water flow over the rocks. Breathing in the afternoon air. Opening myself to the peaceful energy.

I closed my eyes and asked spirit for help. It seemed that I'd been rushing, not able to slow down.

Leaving my clothes on a rock, I dipped into the running water. Its energy surged through me, making me feel alive again.

Spirit, I'm ready to learn the truth from my past lives, so that I can complete the lessons. I am ready to go slow. I am ready to listen to my body. Thank you, spirit.

Inside of me I heard the answers come one by one: Move your body at the speed that you can accept truth.

Finished with my dip, I sat back against a tree to feel the energy of these words.

Ah, I see! I was so excited to meet Roo that I forced my way through experiences and ignored the lessons. Not leaving time and space for integration. Not leaving time to heal. Not seeing emotions as important.

I closed my eyes and felt my heart again. I took a deep breath. Thank you, spirit.

Listening to my body, it wanted more water and less thinking, so I jumped back in to take a refreshing dip.

* * *

Later, back at the house, another truth came: Move in balance. Let your body, mind and spirit move together, led by the heart.

I stopped what I was doing and closed my eyes. Thank you, spirit.

Inhale. Exhale.

Inhale. Exhale.

Yes! I accept balance in my life. I accept the natural rhythm and flow directed by spirit.

* * *

Just before bed, one more gem revealed: Ask each part of you to speak in unison. It's the way to go back home.

Tears filled my eyes. I wanted to go home. I was ready to listen, to hear and feel their truth.

I closed my eyes once again and welcomed all of me back home.

Chapter 6

Jasmine Rain

Light showers fell outside. I could hear the melodic drips as they hit the ground.

This month began with rain, a cleansing of the earth, a cleansing of my spirit.

I took a deep breath. My body wanted to stand in the rain and feel the ground.

I stepped out the door, entering into a misty world, the moisture refreshing my skin.

I wondered now about Roo. It was as if she was in the air, like maybe she was the rain. Another deep breath. My spirit called me to enter the forest.

The rain seemed to wash my insides, bringing peace and soothing away imbalance.

A sweet scent captured my inhalation...a scent that I unknowingly recognized and won't ever forget. The scent of jasmine mixed with rain.

* * *

The forest floor was covered with mossy rocks. My skin felt warm and something stirred inside me. As I walked I could feel that I was not alone. I was surrounded by light energy. It seemed that there were thousands of beings following and guiding me.

Above me all the trees were covered in dewdrops. The sun was out just enough to make them twinkle like Christmas lights. I stopped to feel my heart opening up and radiating outward. My energy focused. I felt solid in a new way.

Usually my thoughts wandered about, thinking of Roo or wondering what was next. In this moment, I felt that everything was okay, exactly as it should be.

I felt peaceful.

* * *

Tonight was the night of Seranga's party. Every year she put together a 'stepping into winter' fiesta. People would come to dance, sing, play music, eat and celebrate the vibrant season ahead.

Some guests wore costumes of weather related things, like icicles or snowflakes. This year I decided to show up dressed as me. That in itself being something to celebrate. I had really come into my own power lately, listening to spirit and my body, following my heart.

Soni and Raji were going as well. I hadn't seen a lot of them lately. The timing was for other things at the moment. It would be good to see them. Part of me really missed hanging out with Soni. We never lacked in adventure!

I was going alone and for the first time, I was okay with that. Roo was in my heart, a part of me, there was nothing to miss.

* * *

Seranga answered the door dressed in a pixie outfit, looking like she was dipped in silver glitter, her pixie wings glistening. She gave a big hug and welcomed me in. The party had already started. Friends were dancing and laughing, lights from above changed colors frequently, red to blue to green and back to red again. It made the room look like a rainbow.

I saw Soni walking toward me, his dark hair spiked and silvery. Raji now rather round, looked like a pregnant snow angel.

"Hey brother!" they said in unison. "Did you just get here?"

Raji added, "This is supposed to be the night of our lives!" holding up her virgin punch.

I felt a calm inside that I'd never experienced. It left me feeling there was nothing to say.

I sat back watching everyone dance, listening to the music, drinking in the experiences. Usually I would be dancing, too, but tonight felt different. I felt different.

In this space, there was nothing to *do*.

* * *

As the evening went on, I began to feel that it was nearly time for me to go. I found Soni and Raji sitting in a corner with a friend. I said my goodbyes and went off to find Seranga. With a hug, I thanked her for inviting me.

When I turned around to head for the door, I saw them, eyes that looked like two deep pools filled with light...drawing me near...

Roo!

Chapter 7

Roo'kystana

My core started shaking as I crossed the sea of dancing people to meet her. She remained still, holding my gaze. She sparkled from the inside out making my heart leap.

"Roo?" I asked aloud, barely breathing.

A long silence passed between us and then: "Yes," she replied.

Electric energy surged through me as I stood there, unsure what else to say, unsure of what to do. Her stare went right through me, as if peaking into my soul and bursting it open wide.

The noise from the music became an echo in the background, drowned out by the beating of my heart.

Finally, I asked: "Would you like to dance?"

Part of me thought that was the dumbest thing to suggest, the other part felt like holding her, to the sweet music of my love.

She nodded her head once and I took her hand leading us to the dance floor.

I wondered if I even knew how to dance. I wondered if my feet were even on the floor.

As we swayed in the middle of this vast group of other people, I noticed how radiant she was. Her beautiful pools of light blinked rarely, but when they did they seemed to affect the lighting in the room. Her long hair, the color of snow, gently fell over her shoulders.

Her presence was innocent and peaceful, her energy reminded me of soft clouds.

It was as if there was no one else in the room, just the two of us dancing.

* * *

Soni approached with a look of absolute pleasure on his face. He stopped a few feet in front of us and stared. He said nothing and stared.

I looked over at him, and then went back to feeling Roo.

The rest of the world melted away when she was there.

The hours passed so quickly holding Roo and dancing. I turned my head and noticed that the room was basically empty. A few people were by the juice bar chatting with Seranga.

I shook myself like a dog, trying to reset.

And then asked: "Roo, do you want to come home?"

Come home? What was I saying, she'd never been there before, we just met this evening, how could I be so bold?

"Yes," she said softly.

Wow! She has no fear. I'm shaking from my words and she lets them roll off of her so easily. How does she do it?

That's right, she's part of me, too.

* * *

When we arrived at home, I asked her if she would like a walk.

Telepathically she answered: 'Yes.'

Our energy together was so serene, almost like we were in another world. She said very little, but what she said was so clear and true.

We walked around back by the pine trees. I showed her my favorite stars through my telescope and shared what I had named them.

"Over there, that's Trixie and do you see that one, it just blinked, that's Jerome."

I was so close to her skin, she smelled sweet like a flower. As I spoke to her, she looked deep into my eyes, a tender smile on her face.

I shivered just being near her.

It started to get a bit cold outside so I invited her in to sit by a nice fire. She pulled me closer and together we walked inside.

I asked: "Roo, would you like a cup of herbal tea?"

She hopped up next to me and pressed her wet, warm lips on my cheek. It felt like a bolt of lightning hit me, my whole body became electrified!

The cup that I had been holding in my hand fell, heading for the floor. Just before the cup hit, she caught it, seemingly without effort.

My eyes wide with disbelief, I stared at her without blinking.

She handed me the cup: "Here, my love." Out popped a giggle and she walked away.

* * *

When I finished heating the tea, I turned around and she was dancing and twirling about the living room...two feet off the ground!

She transmitted telepathically: 'Don't drop the cup,' and giggled again.

I laughed out loud and released a tight spot in my chest where I'd been holding on.

I took a deep breath. I want to play, too!

We danced and played for half the night. She invited over pixies and fairies and a gnome called Sireal. Everyone played hide and seek, ring around the rosie, and a bunch of other games that we made up. I never laughed so much in my life. The energy was so high, that anything seemed possible. And yet it was so calm and real that it felt balanced.

Finally, after the last game of tug-a-peace with Sireal, I was tired and ready for sleep. The whole gang, pixies, fairies, Sireal, Roo and I curled up on the soft rug next to the fireplace and drifted into dreams.

* * *

It was a chilly morning and I rolled over trying to pull the blanket closer. I opened my eyes to see Roo like a cloud napping in mid air, and a pixie was asleep on my nose.

After moving the pixie, I sat up to stretch myself awake. Inhale. Exhale. Inhale. Exhale. Then I went to the kitchen to whip up a smoothie. I noticed something out of the corner of my eye. It was Sireal. He was outside making snow gnomes!

I finished making the smoothie and brought a glass for Roo. She was already down from her sleeping spot, sitting in front of the fire.

"It snowed last night, Roo. Did you see?" I asked, offering her a smoothie.

She glanced over at me holding the glass.

'Thank you,' she transmitted.

I looked down at my hand and stood there in disbelief. The glass was empty and clean.

What will happen next?

Chapter 8
Zephyr Winds

The days went on and I began to wonder if I deserved such a magical, beautiful creature such as Roo. I felt so Earthly, so caught up in my ways. She ran around having fun and creating adventure, things that I've never even thought of. Not that I wasn't happy having her here, I love having her here with me, I love her ways.

I just wasn't sure about me.

We were on a nature walk in the snow, when I asked her: "Roo, it's great being together right now, it's so precious to me. But I couldn't help wondering when you have to leave and go home."

I couldn't believe that I was asking! I've waited forever to find her and now I want to know when she's leaving? Argh!

"I am home, silly," and she threw another snowball.

Great, now you're not making her feel welcome. Way to go.

"Oh, of course this is your home, too, but I meant your other home. You know where you keep your things."

There I said it.

Her big eyes blinked once and she cocked her head to the side.

"Things?" she said aloud.

I waited awhile and then bravely asked: "Roo, where did you come from? I mean we met at the party, where were you just before that?"

"Ooh!!" she said as if she just figured out what I was talking about.

And then, she did the one thing that I didn't understand, she pointed up toward the sky!

* * *

We got back to the house and sat down by the cozy fire. My core felt cold.

I sat quiet for a long time and then: "Roo?"

"Yes, snowy robin?" she blinked again and smiled.

God, she was amazing. The way she spoke and the sweetness in her smile. How could I even think of her leaving? Why am I being so difficult?

I paused.

"Roo, I love you..." I began.

"I love you, too, my little snow-mallow," she said giving me a moist kiss on my forehead.

Electricity ran through me again, like sparklers were going off inside me.

"Roo, I love you and I want to spend time with you, but right now I need some time to myself. You know to think."

Oh, no what was I doing. I'm going to hurt her.

"Okay, muffin," she kissed my nose and with a hop she was gone from the room.

* * *

As cold as it was, I needed to go sit by my favorite tree. My heart sank wondering if I was ruining the most beautiful experience I've ever had.

I put a mat down on the ground and sat to meditate. I crossed my legs, closed my eyes, took a deep breath, and focused on my heart.

Immediately, Roo's face popped up in front of me. Her smile and all the sweetness about her.

I refocused and began opening my heart again.

The sound of her laughter filled the air.

I started to weep. Tears streamed down my cheeks, making little icicles on my face. I cried harder, from my belly. Deep rolling sobs came from within. The tears now gushing, as if a water dam just broke.

Oh, spirit! I said aloud. I feel so lost!

What happened, I cried. What is happening to me?

* * *

When I finally returned to the house after meditating and a walk, it had been a couple of hours. I felt better, though not completely resolved. The crying helped.

I went to go find her, to apologize, but she was gone.

I sat on the floor next to the fire and cried again.

"Who am I?" I said aloud.

"You're snow-butterfly!" she said with a giggle. In a moment she hopped on my lap and kissed my lips. Tingles ran through me in waves. It felt as though my cells were filling with light and rejuvenating. And my breathing was deep and rhythmic.

Slowly, she moved back from my face, just enough to look at me, to look in my eyes.

"Snow-bear, I love you," she said tenderly, melting the ice and snow within me.

Tears like little dewdrops rolled down my cheeks.

"You love me?" I asked practically sobbing. "Why?"

"You know why, silly," she replied, rubbing noses with me. "I am you," Roo pressed her light, airy body against mine hugging my soul, healing my wounds and loving my spirit.

I am you.

Chapter 9

Choosing Love

Though I tried to ignore it, I just couldn't. She was flipping my world inside out, in every way. Who knew finding the love to live for would be so drastic and feel so crazy.

It was time to call in some help before I scared her away for good. Or ran away!

"Hey brother!" I said calling Soni.

"Brother, brother, brother," he said in return.

"My brother..." I replied back.

"Brother...?" he said beginning to question the nature of my call.

"Brother...I..." I tried again.

Then finally: "Hey what's going on over there? You sound like you're in trouble?"

Soni always knew the truth.

Without another response from me, he said: "I'm coming over there. We'll go out for a while. See you in a few," and he hung up the phone.

* * *

We sat at a table in the local coffee shop, sipping chai and talking.

"Soni, you don't understand, she's amazing, the most amazing being that I've ever met...but I'm going crazy...where is she from...what is she doing here.... I mean she sleeps on the ceiling for goodness sake.... it's beautiful don't get me wrong, but...I mean I can't do that.... what does she want from me...maybe I could learn how to do certain things...but the gnomes..."

At this point, Soni interrupted.

"Gnomes??" he looked like he just swallowed wrong.

"Yes, gnomes...and pixies and fairies.... we go for walks and the bears follow us...it's weird...I mean it's fantastic...but I've never had bears following me.... and then to top it all off, she is always telling me she loves me...no matter what.... I mean what...."

He interrupted again.

"Wait a minute, brother, telling you she loves you cannot be your biggest problem. Slow down for a minute and listen to yourself."

Authority had spoken. And I sat back in my chair.

* * *

"Brother," Soni began after some time passed. "What have you wanted your whole life, really? You've always spoken of desiring a love to live for. Who cares how she sleeps? Isn't she what you asked for?"

He had a point.

Soni continued: "Then what are you afraid of?"

"I'm scared that I'm not good enough!" I blurted out. "I'm scared she's going to leave when she finds out who I really am. Just plain old boring me."

"Love doesn't work that way, brother," Soni replied. "She loves you exactly for who you are."

I just sat there, trying to drink in his words, unable to swallow them.

Then at last: "Hey brother, why don't you and Roo come over tonight? We'll have dinner and then go soak in the tub next door."

Yes, that sounded good. I nodded my head approvingly.

As he dropped me off at my house, his parting words were: "So what do you want to do, choose fear or choose love?" and he drove away.

Mmmm....that's right...

I choose love.

Chapter 10

Letting Go

The rest of the afternoon, I was quiet. Contemplating life and Soni's words. Roo on the other hand was sprinkling the whole house in pixie dust. She was laughing and playing, singing and dancing with the fairies and pixies. They had even invited in an opossum family, a raccoon and a bird that decided not to fly south.

This is exactly what worried me.

What was going to happen when we were around others? They are going to think she is crazy, not normal somehow. I didn't want her to get hurt.

I didn't want to lose my friends.

Just before we left to meet up with Soni and Raji, I said: "Hey, could we leave the animals and fairies behind?"

"Oh good idea, we'll have a treat and bring the pixies," she gave me a kiss on the cheek.

That wasn't what I had in mind.

"And the pixies, Roo. I was wondering if we could go, just the two of us. Is that okay?" I asked hopefully.

She nodded yes and we got in the truck.

* * *

We arrived at about 5pm. Soni came out to greet us.

"Hey sister, nice to meet you!" he gave her a warm welcoming hug.

She smiled and stared into his eyes. Soni began to smile, too, a melty kind of smile as if was drugged with a happiness pill.

Strange. I thought to myself. I hope this was a good idea.

Raji came out just then: "Hey Roo, we've been waiting to meet you." She gave Roo a hug and kissed her cheek.

Roo blinked and smiled showing all of her pretty white teeth. Soni and Raji looked at each other longingly, held hands and turned to walk inside.

"I love you, baby," I heard Soni say to Raji as they walked through the front door.

Roo and I followed them in. But their behavior was rather suspicious.

* * *

Soni served us iced tea out in the back yard and went back inside. The two of them returned within a minute with fruit salad, raw veggie burgers, carrot sticks with a chickpea dip, and set the table.

That was fast, I thought.

The whole time we were eating Soni and Raji were feeding each other morsels and practically rubbing noses. Soni kept rubbing her round belly and talking to it in an altered voice.

"How is daddy's little bundle of joy? Goochee, goochee, goo."

Raji was glowing, letting everyone know each time the baby kicked.

Goochee, goochee, goo? I'd never seen them like this before.

After dinner, Soni cleared away the dishes, telling Raji to sit and relax. Raji just looked at him and smiled. Then turned her gaze toward Roo and I, the smile stayed as she said: "I am the luckiest girl ever, don't you think?"

Roo nodded a big nod and vibrantly said: "Yes!"

I didn't say a word.

We headed over to Solana's place next door to soak in the hot tub. Solana's fiancé was there; usually he was out of town on business.

Solana practically ran up to Roo and hugged her like they were long lost friends.

"Roo! I'm so happy that you came!" another big hug.

She pointed to her fiancé, then said: "And this is Greg."

Greg walked over to shake my hand like usual, instead gave both of us a hug. Sure it was the kind where the guy slaps your back, but still.

What was going on? I had never seen him like this.

* * *

Everyone was getting in the tub, except Raji who was sitting out and dipping her feet in.

When Roo suddenly took off all her clothes and hopped in.

No one even noticed!

Well, I noticed.

But the rest of the gang seemed completely oblivious to this.

What is going on? I said to myself again. Am I dreaming?

Somebody pinch me.

"Ouch!" I shrieked aloud.

Roo had pinched my leg under the water.

I said telepathically: 'Why did you do that?'

Her transmitted reply: 'Because you asked me to.'

I needed to remember that, she could hear my thoughts.

* * *

Later back at the house, Roo said: "I had a wonderful time just the two of us. Thank you warm and snowy bunny," she gave me the longest sweetest kiss we'd ever shared so far. The hair on the back of my neck stood on end and my pockets turned inside out.

I need to let go, I thought to myself.

Spirit, I want that. I am ready to just let go...

Chapter 11
Time To Go Slow

I approached Roo with a smile and a kiss.

"Roo, I would like to talk. There are some things that I really need to share with you."

"Okay," she replied gently.

We sat in the living room by the fire. It would have been easier to be outside sitting on the ground if today wasn't so cold.

I made us both a warm mug of tea and sat back down.

"Roo, I've been feeling crazy since we met. In lots of good ways, but also lots of ways that didn't feel balanced for me." I took a sip of tea and continued: "I love how spontaneous you are and how you take naps and the way you look upside down, standing on the ceiling. I love our home sprinkled in pixie dust and filled with furry friends. I love how you walk into a room and change everyone's life...for the better."

She smiled at me and blinked once changing the lighting in the room.

I kept on going: "But I was afraid that those magical qualities would drive people away from us. Then I remembered back to when my parents were alive. You would have liked them, Roo, they were kindhearted people, they loved nature and the Earth. The thing is they were not comfortable with the magical world we live in now. It scared them."

I paused for a moment, giving space for my words and my feelings.

"Roo, when I was younger, I used to play outside with fairies and salamanders. I used to talk to the birds and I was friends with the trees. I began to share my adventures with my parents, thinking they would be happy and want to play with me. But they didn't. They told me to stop. They said it wasn't right and that I was hurting myself by believing in these made up friends."

My eyes were filled with tears.

"Roo, I took on their fears. I didn't even realize it until you and I met. These fears belong to them and I'm ready to give them back, every last fear." I started to shake from the power in my words.

Aloud I said: "Spirit, I return these fears back to the beings they belong to. I no longer wish to carry around others pain. I am ready to be free!"

The energy started to shift. My body felt lighter. I felt clear.

Roo gave me space and didn't say a word until now.

"Lovey-bear, you are so special to me." Her eyes twinkled and she gave me a hug.

"I want to keep making space for our love, for our life. I say yes to magic! I say yes to us!" I said holding her hand, tears still flowing.

I'm ready.

Chapter 12

A New World

Roo and I were sitting outside under our favorite oak tree meditating. The sun was out and the snow had melted away. Birds were chirping overhead.

We were practicing a sunbeam meditation; our legs crossed, my behind on the ground, hers three feet off the ground!

Our energy together had grown so peaceful over the past several weeks. She didn't scare me anymore and I was accepting more of my own unique abilities.

The meditation was almost complete and we said thank you to the sun. Just then, a small being popped up in front of us.

He greeted us with a bow and said: "My lord and lady of Afaria, I am very pleased to meet with you at last." He finished bowing and looked straight into our eyes. "I am Aquisarthynon."

Roo and I exchanged glances, telepathically asking each other: 'Who?'

Roo gave him a smile, a big wide smile before saying: "Why, AQ, I almost didn't recognize you and what's with the long name," she began giggling.

Huh? Who is AQ? I wondered.

"My lord," Roo said to me. "AQ is a fellow Afarian. He's here to help the planet, just like us."

Huh? I said to myself. But she heard me anyway.

"Afaria is where we came from. I know you don't remember. You've been here too long. But it's true."

"Okay," I replied, remembering to just let go. "Welcome AQ! And what brings you here on this fine day?"

AQ addressed me again: "My lord, I am here to reactivate your Afarian memory, a.k.a. to give you the AM. Roo came straight down, so she is still activated. You on the other hand need a boost," he said with a laugh.

"Will it hurt?" I asked.

"No, no, it won't hurt a bit. Here close your eyes," AQ motioned to me.

I looked at Roo once more. "Is everything okay?" I asked.

"Yes, love," she blinked once and I shut my eyes.

* * *

When I woke from a dreamy space, my head felt a little funny. Roo was sitting there next to me, smiling.

"Hi, love," she said to me, one blink and I felt normal again.

"I remember!" I said. "I remember our purpose!"

I could feel the energy welling up inside me.

Somewhere in the sky, we could hear clapping, as if the Afarians were all listening delightfully. Roo smiled and urged me to say more.

"We came here to bring the inhabitants of the planet together, to construct a web of peace. We are bridging the way between animals, people, fairies, pixies, gnomes, bugs...you name it!" I continued: "I came ahead to do research. This whole time, I had a part of me that was copying or memorizing the lay of the land and patterns on the planet! I remember now! I remember it all!"

I gave Roo a long hug. Then I looked into her eyes without blinking and gave her a kiss. I heard explosions above us, like rockets or fireworks, everything looked clear and bright and my pockets all turned inside out!

"Roo, I remember who I am!"

Part II
Call Of The Earth And Her Children

Contents

Chapter 1

Spinning Spheres

Planets were swirling above my head, twisting and rotating around each other. The moon was in the middle like a huge sphere of light. Like a flash I could view from inside the sphere. A person was standing there, surrounded by twelve smaller spinning spheres. Each one a different color, each one energetically unique.

I heard the words: We are all one.

I awoke in a sweat, taking a deep breath.

Turning my head quickly, I saw Roo sleeping midair next to me.

I heard her say: "We are all one. We are all one."

Shivers ran through me and I woke her up.

"Roo, wake up, we need to talk," I said gently nudging her.

Telepathically she transmitted: 'The Earth is calling us. Are you ready?'

Calling us? Part of me still wondered what that meant.

"Yes," I replied aloud. "I am ready."

Just then the energy shifted and a strong wind swirled around us. In a blink of the eye, we were whisked from there.

Another journey began.

* * *

My heart sank. The Earth was in trouble and I had been so detached from her troubles. Roo and I lived in harmony with Mother Earth, right there in our own yard. The rest of the planet struggles as I sit in my separate paradise.

A voice spoke to me: Come help my children before it is too late.

To myself, I said: We are coming!

In the next moment, we found ourselves driving in the truck down a long, dusty road. It was barren land except for a rickety wooden fence along the edge of the road and an occasional house. Even the houses looked rickety, like no one lived there for years.

I felt sad and a bit dusty.

"Roo, where are we?" I asked aloud.

"She is calling us to a place down the way from here. They need help."

Help? I wondered. I didn't feel ready to help, not knowing what that means.

In about ten minutes we were led down another small road, to the left of the one we had been on. There were no trees in sight and the earth was dry.

Where was all the water? I wondered. Weren't there any streams?

We pulled up to a small white house, a few trees around it, probably for shade.

I didn't know why we were there, but I got out anyway.

Roo walked up to the door, just as an older man opened it. She smiled her big wide smile and blinked.

"Why, hello," he said. "It's hotter than the dickens out here, why don't you all come inside." The man turned to go back in and motioned for us to follow.

Gee, she is amazing! I thought and followed her into the house.

* * *

"Please have a seat," the man said. "Can I get you anything?"

Roo stared at him, her two beautiful pools of light swirling.

"Where is the water?" she asked finally.

Oh, that's a good idea, I thought. I could use a drink of water.

"Come with me," he said. "It's out in the back."

Roo and I followed him out the back door and into the heat. We walked past the hills framing his home and saw a grove of trees! There was green everywhere!

"About a year ago the water in these parts just dried up," the man said to us. "All that's left is this little spring right here." He pointed to the pool of water surrounded by trees.

Roo walked over to the water's edge and knelt down next to it. She touched her small fingers against the water. As she did not only did ripples radiate through the water, but Roo lit up! Her whole body, radiating rosy light around her.

She began communicating telepathically with the land. I could hear her soft whisper chanting energetic rhythms into the earth, reminding it of its purpose.

The earth started to move and shift, more water spouted out of the ground. Within minutes there was a narrow waterway flowing about a mile long, on past the man's house.

He looked at her with a crooked, toothy smile, eyes wet with tears. "Why thank you, ma'am. I don't know how to ever repay you."

She smiled and gave his wet cheek a kiss.

Gently the words flowed from her: "We are all one."

One blink and we were gone.

* * *

Next we watched a scene from a distance: There was a family sitting inside their home. The mother and father were talking about their daughter. They were worried about her safety when she goes outside and at the same time concerned about how sad she is being kept inside. The mother was crying and asking for help. The girl was sitting in the other room staring out the window.

"I'm afraid she'll get hurt," said the mother. "Yesterday she wandered off into the forest by herself, before I had a chance to see where she went. Anything could happen."

Suddenly, we were dropped into a field of flowers. There were multi-colored butterflies everywhere we looked. Songbirds filled the air.

Up ahead was the same girl, playing on the grass. Light transmitted from her eyes as she telepathically drew in animals, gnomes, fairies and birds. Even the trees and flowers seemed to move closer to her.

Roo skipped over and sat down next to the girl. She blinked her big eyes and communicated silently with the child.

'I am lonely,' telepathed the girl.

'You are never alone,' Roo transmitted, gently placing her hand over the girl's heart.

'They don't understand me,' replied the girl.

Roo blinked twice, something I never saw her do, light flashed from her eyes.

Reality seemed to change. It melted away and reformed itself right in front of us.

Did she just alter reality? I wondered.

"We are all one," said Roo in the air.

When I looked up, the girl was walking away, birds and butterflies around her, she was holding hands with someone.... it was her mother! Her father ran up the hill toward them and gave her a kiss.

The three of them turned around and smiled.

"Thank you," the girl said, light transmitting from her eyes.

In a moment we were gone.

Chapter 2

Home Again

I need to slow down, I thought to myself.

Immediately, we reappeared in the truck, a few miles from the house. I was driving and in familiar territory.

I breathed a sigh of relief.

I had been feeling the need to go slow, to put my feet back on the ground.

Things had been going so fast lately. I wasn't even sure how to stop moving or how to communicate what I needed.

But luckily we were on our way home now.

I was so amazed by everything that just happened, the way we traveled and how Roo healed people and the earth so easily. But wow, it kind of blew me away.

I was feeling overwhelmed and unsure.

"Roo, I'm a bit dizzy from all of this experience. I think I need some time to recover," I said aloud.

She smiled her bright beautiful smile and said: "Okay, spring bunny." With a kiss to my cheek, she hopped up and flew away.

What do I do to recover? I thought.

Just then, the phone rang. It was Soni.

"Hey brother, you want to go for a hike? It's a perfect day out there," said Soni.

A hike, I thought, that's exactly what I needed!

"Sure, love to," I replied with excitement.

"I'll pick you up in a few," he replied.

* * *

"You see, I've been feeling completely overwhelmed," I was saying to Soni as we walked out of the parking area to find a trail. "One minute we were in our house, the next thing I know we are driving down a dusty road to meet an old man and fix his water problem."

I paused, "That's the other thing, Roo knows exactly what she's doing. She asked the man about the water, and I thought she meant a drink. How did she know what we were there for? I felt like I was falling behind."

Just then, a baby bird fell out of its nest. I jumped over to catch it.

Tucking the bird into my pocket, I pulled myself up into the tree, found the nest, and returned him safely to it.

There you go little fella, I transmitted.

"Um..."Soni tried to speak.

"Anyway," I continued. "What is my part in all of this? What are my gifts..." I stopped and sniffed the air, then made a sudden turn to the left. "Let's get some of the berries that are over there," I said.

Within a minute we found a patch of berries, not visible from the trail we were on.

"Um..." began Soni.

I cut him off: "Where was I? Oh yeah, I feel like I should have answers and maybe I do, but I don't know what they are. It's frustrating. I feel so disconnected."

"Oh, let's go take a dip in the creek," I said leading Soni down a path we'd not been on before. After a while, we heard the sound of the water flowing over rocks. It was the creek.

"Um..." Soni tried again.

"Right, as I was saying, what is my purpose, what are my gifts, I need to know."

I stopped and sat down by the water, taking a deep breath.

Soni plopped down next to me, mouth open, unable to speak.

* * *

"What is it, Soni? Did you want to say something?"

Soni re-centered himself, and replied: "Yes. Yes I do. Last night I had this crazy dream and you were in it. I was struggling in my relationship with Raji, the baby was coming and as I experienced things in the dream, different parts of me expressed themselves. Like in one scene Raji was standing in the kitchen, asking for help, I switched into another part of myself and flew into the kitchen. Then another scene, the baby was talking to me from inside of Raji and I could hear her! It was like I had all these abilities that I wasn't aware of. It was beginning to freak me out." He paused. "Then you came in and showed me who I am, using this big bubble thing. I was inside and you walked me through using it."

Inside a big bubble? I thought. Is he talking about the sphere?

Soni continued: "That's the strange thing, today as we were hiking, you unknowingly healed these parts of me that felt separate...just by actions that you took with your body."

"What do you mean?" I asked, wanting to know more.

"First, when we were hiking, I heard this baby bird cry out. At first I didn't know what I was hearing. Then, you jumped over and caught the bird! It was then that I realized what I heard was real!"

"Oh, just like the ability you had in your dream to hear the baby talk inside Raji!" I said, getting shivers.

"Exactly!" he replied. "Thank you so much, brother. You have no idea how much it helped me." Soni looked over at me and smiled.

I thought for a moment, then shared my dream with Soni.

"Soni last night I had a dream, too."

"I'm listening," he said looking intently at me.

"It had a large swirling sphere with a person inside, you know like a bubble. Surrounding them were twelve smaller, colored spheres. You see in your dream you were shown how your body was meant to work, without Earthly limitations. You could fly and play with time, even communicate with your unborn child. But while you are awake you are streamlining your thoughts through one part of you. Most people do that, it's more comfortable for them. When we were first born, we used all parts of ourselves. Over time things happened causing us to reject parts. In your case, you are funneling your experience through one sphere, over here," I said pointing to the placement of a dark colored sphere to his left. "You need to say yes to the other parts of you, listen to them and welcome them back home." I sat back against the tree next to me.

"Wow, I didn't know I knew all that! It just came to me when you mentioned your dream! Crazy, huh?" I said to Soni.

"Yeah, crazy," he said leaning back to lie on the ground.

Just then, Roo's face flashed in front of me and I heard her say: 'We are all one.'

"Did you say something, brother?" replied Soni.

I laughed to myself.

Chapter 3
Following Footsteps

Footsteps lined along the row
Of places where I'd want to go
Visions held they were so grand
The answers all within my hand
Truth inside a swirling sphere
Help to release all of my fear
Mirrors seen in your eyes
Creating peace and making ties

* * *

The evening came and Roo and I sat in our favorite tree to enjoy the sky. She was draped over a big sturdy branch, looking upward. I was leaning back against the upper trunk of the tree, her tiny feet in my lap.

"Roo," I said at last. "Do you believe in magic?"

Okay, what was going on with me.... did she believe in magic?? She is magic!

She kept her gaze up toward the stars and the dark misty sky.

"Roo," I tried again. "Do you think it's possible to know things without knowing that you know them?"

Blah, I thought to myself. What am I really trying to say?

Silence filled the air.

"Roo," I began. This time she sat up and looked into my eyes. "Roo, I'm scared."

"Ooh, honey bear, I love you." She gave me a kiss like never before. My hair stood up, electricity ran through me and I started to cry.

"I love you, too," I said through my tears.

She held me in her arms, warming me, allowing me space to release my fears.

Something inside me shifted, the fear I had about who I am and what I know practically vanished. I no longer felt the need to speak words or explain anything. I just let Roo hold me. I let the walls melt away.

* * *

The morning light was now shining in the bedroom window and I stretched my spirit awake.

Boy, I could use a soak in the water. I thought to myself.

And bam! Just like that I was in the bathtub, covered in warm bubbly water.

At first it was rather shocking and then I kind of got used to the idea.

Well, I did want water.

I closed my eyes, allowing the warmth to relax me.

I'm thirsty, I thought. I'd love a smoothie.

Next thing I know I'm dried, dressed and standing in the kitchen with a tall glass of smoothie in my hand.

I laughed aloud.

Oh, and I would like Roo to be here as well.

Pop! Roo was sitting on the counter, smiling at me.

"Hi, honey bee!" she said.

My head started to get dizzy, so I thought I should go sit down on the couch, this time walking there myself.

"Roo, I'm scared again. I think I need some help."

* * *

"Hello, sir," said a voice.

I turned and saw a small being next to me.

AQ!

"Why AQ, you have perfect timing, I was just asking for help," I said aloud, "Maybe I need another reactivation or something."

"My lord, you require an upgrade to your crystalline sphere. As with most Earth beings, your sphere got cracked along the way. It is time to repair it and realign all your other spheres."

"Oh, you mean like in the dream I had? There were twelve smaller spheres inside the big one, is that right?" I asked, excited that I knew what he was talking about.

"Yes, my lord, that's correct. The small spheres are aspects of you. They create experiences that are part of your path or purpose." He paused. "Fear and trauma cause your spheres to misalign. Once misaligned they crack the crystalline sphere that keeps you on your purpose."

Wow, I had no idea. That's probably why I've been feeling so strange.

"Are you ready for your repair, sir?" asked AQ.

"Yes, I'm ready."

* * *

I drifted off into a dreamy space where I could hear voices talking about my spheres.

"His sphere number four needs repair," said one of the voices.

"Yes. It looks like it became misaligned when he was three years old. He was using his ability to alter time, which scared his mother. She took him to the doctor for an examination to make sure nothing was 'wrong' with him. The whole event caused him to believe he was wrong for using this ability and wrong for being himself," the other voice said. "We'll readjust the vibration of the sphere and bring healing to the memory."

"Okay, he also needs his number seven sphere repaired. It's full of dust," said the first voice.

"Beginning repair to number seven. It looks like he brought this one with him from a past life experience. The lesson in that lifetime was to follow your heart. He didn't quite learn that, so the lesson followed him. We are now adjusting the frequency of the sphere to level 10 and clearing the dust. Full knowledge of the completed lesson will be available for him," said the other voice.

A different voice entered in. It was softer and lighter. "Please reconnect his chakras to the adjoining spheres and format his experience to match the adjustments." The voice paused, as if thinking something over.

"Adjust the energy frequency for each spine connector and repair the crystalline sphere. Good work, beings. We'll talk more once you are finished."

With that the voices were silent and I slipped into a deeper state of dream.

Chapter 4

A New Spring

I could see the light from behind my closed lids. It must be morning, I thought.

My eyes barely open a crack, I tried to get up, then flopped back down on the bed.

Oh my gosh, what happened to me? I wondered.

I tried again to open my eyes, my lids were heavy and what I could see was blurry.

"Roo?" I called out into the blurry shadows.

"Yes, lovey-bunny?" I heard her sweet voice respond from the abyss.

"I can't see. Can you see me?" I asked.

"Sweet honey berry, everything is fine. And yes I can see you."

Her words were comforting, but I still felt quite odd.

"My head feels like a balloon on a string floating above my shoulders," I complained. "Are you sure this is normal?"

Roo just giggled.

I could feel her gently stroking my face and hair. She was whispering something.... a song maybe. It sounded beautiful. I let myself get lost in the melody and drifted back into dreams.

* * *

I'm not sure what time of day it was when I finally got up. Everything seemed foggy.

Roo was already outside. I could hear her singing.

Gently, I got up, still a bit sore from all of the adjusting that happened yesterday. As I walked downstairs, I noticed that I could feel my crystalline sphere around me! I had never experienced that before.

It would be easier to just be outside already, I thought.

And bip! I was outside with Roo.

A giggle popped out.

Roo was up in the tree again. I watched her decorating it with fairy dust, doing her part to help the spring leaves and buds grow.

I thought, I'd love to be up there in the tree with Roo.

Bop! There I was, sitting on Roo's lap in the tree.

"Hi honey top!" said Roo with a laugh. She gave me a big hug and kissed me. I laughed, too.

This time I wasn't scared.

* * *

We stayed in the tree for quite a while, enjoying the warm sunshine. It was peaceful today, inside and out. As I rested there, my head on Roo's lap, she stroked my face. Just like last night.

"Would you like a walk, bunny love?" she asked.

I thought for a moment, then: "Yes, that sounds nice."

"You know it was weird," I began. "Soni and I were hiking the other day and I adjusted time to catch a baby bird that was falling from its nest. It helped Soni wake up more of himself, too. When I used to do things like that, I got dragged into the doctors office to check my sanity." I laughed, thinking about how much I've grown.

Roo and I walked hand in hand in the yard toward the back woods. I could really feel the crystalline sphere now. It felt warm and full around me, like I was nestled into the womb again. Everything feels possible.

I led us into the forest and through the trees, like a light was guiding me. We turned this way and that, around bushes and branches with ease.

I felt lighter inside.

About a mile into the walk, I led us to a small spring and waterfall, one that I had never been to. In fact I've walked this land many times before and I'd not seen it.

Roo was so excited, she just took off her dress to dance under the falling water. She made it look fun and inviting. In a moment I was dancing under the fall with her, the sun shining down on us.

I felt strong again.

"Roo I'm in love!" I said my eyes wide.

This time I communicated with more than words, I sent my energy to her, wrapping sweetness and love around her. Something I'd never done before...never felt I could do.

"I love you, Roo. I love me. I love our life...I love it all!!" A smile washed over me.

Roo smiled, too.

Chapter 5
Things To Come

The early evening sky was splashed in soft pink, yellow and blue. Roo was floating above the ground, like a fairy, her long misty hair sparkling. It was peaceful.

Suddenly, the wind whipped up and practically blew me over, leaves spiraled in the air.

"It's time," I said.

With that, we were gone.

We reappeared in the truck driving toward a town. I could see buildings and hills in the distance. The land looked green, with lots of different trees. The sun was shining.

Roo was singing quietly: "Aria-non, Ari-an-on..." Goosebumps covered me, head to toe.

Wherever we were going, it was big!

* * *

I pulled the truck into a long driveway, the sign on the corner said 'Mineral Springs Park'. Up ahead there were flowers and grassy fields.

I wondered if we had been here before, it felt familiar. Chills ran up my back.

Once the truck was parked, I led us over to an open field to sit down.

I heard a voice whispering: The light you will remember.

My whole body shook. Energy ran through me.

Another gust of wind, blowing our hair about.

"Over here," I said to Roo, leading her up the hill.

When we got to the top, I saw a picture flash of a little girl. She had birds, fairies, some small animals and two gnomes playing with her. She was laughing as the birds untied her shoelaces. Light beaming from her eyes.

It was the same girl we visited before!

I wonder why we are back here? I thought.

The image of the girl now faded, leaving just the grass, flowers and Roo.

"Roo, what just happened?" I asked.

"Close your eyes, love. You will remember," she said softly.

I closed my eyes and drifted into a new space. I saw the little girl and her parents just like before. The parents were upset, they were afraid. Then we popped over to the grassy spot where Roo and I now stood and watched as all their problems lifted away.

Then I heard a voice: Your experience is not done. It was a preview of what is to come.

A preview? I thought.

"Will we meet this girl then?" I asked the voice.

It replied: When the time is right and still, you will journey there together. Open your heart to the magic inside of you, to the child who longs to play.

With that, we were gone.

* * *

We were now standing by our truck at the ocean.

The air was moist and warm. The sound of waves crashing on the sand filled our ears.

"Where are we?" I wondered aloud.

Roo ran off toward the water and began jumping over waves.

I couldn't seem to relax. I had the feeling that something was about to happen.

My eyes scanned the area, looking for signs. They saw nothing.

I waited to feel the gust of wind, but the air was calm.

So I decided to go find Roo.

"Do you want to go for a walk?" I asked. "I'm feeling nervous and can't find a reason why."

"Sure, honey bee," she said wrapping her arms around my waist.

"I'm not sure why we are here but I can feel the energy going higher and higher. It feels like something is happening." As I spoke these words out loud, my tension eased slightly.

Just then we saw a dog playing in the water. Roo ran toward him. I decided to run there, too.

He bounced over to us, asking for some attention.

I knelt down to pet him. He was soft and brown. His long tongue was hanging out of his mouth and he seemed to be smiling.

His eyes, I said to myself, they look right through me.

"Roo, did you see how awake this dog is?" I asked aloud.

Then feeling a bit nervous again: "I wonder where his owners are?"

* * *

I never had a dog before, I thought to myself.

"Oh, he's so sweet, Roo. Did you see him licking me?"

Roo came over and put her arms around my neck, her deep pools looking into mine.

"I love you, fuzzy bear," she said kissing my lips.

Electricity surged through me, my heart raced, turning my pockets inside out.

It felt nice being here with Roo and the dog, but part of me felt scared.

I took a moment to think.

"Roo, I wasn't allowed to have pets when I was growing up. My parents didn't trust me to take care of them."

Then I looked over at the dog, his doggy tail wagging, a big smile on his furry face.

"It feels like everything is crashing in," I began. "We are popping about, without a chance to even integrate the experiences we're having. I think I need to go back home."

In a blink of the eye, we were driving home.

* * *

We were a few minutes from the house, when I started talking.

"I'm sorry. I didn't want to ruin the fun you were having. I just feel so unresolved inside, about everything."

Roo just smiled at me, her eyes melting away my fears.

"I always wanted a dog, Roo. I wished so many times that I could have one. Every night before I fell asleep, I prayed for a dog." My eyes began tearing up. "But my wish never came true, I could have used a friend."

I was fully crying now, I had to pull over, I couldn't hold it in anymore.

Roo held me in her arms as I released my old wounds.

She whispered softly in the air: "Let it go."

Chapter 6
The Child Within

Roo and I decided to spend the day hiking. There was a 4000 ft mountain close to the house. I put a few things in a pack, some fruit, trail mix, and water, and we were off.

I pulled into the parking area, next to a tree for shade.

This time Roo led the way, choosing a trail...or making a trail, in the direction that she wanted to go.

About an hour in, we came to a crossroads with a larger trail. There was a man and a small boy stopped on the trail.

The man was upset: "I told you not to do that. How many times do I need to say the same thing....?"

Something tightened inside of me.

We crossed the trail and continued up the mountain.

* * *

A while later, the tight feeling came back. It started clogging in my throat.

I saw a picture flash in front of me. It was of the small boy. The man was standing over him yelling.

All of the sudden, I screamed: "Stop it! Leave him alone! He's just a child. Can't you see he's only a child?"

When I turned my head, Roo had stopped and was looking at me, her big beautiful eyes gently watching me.

Feeling afraid still, I said: "What? Didn't you see him? That guy was yelling at the boy, squashing him! Telling him that it's not okay to be playful anymore! It's not okay to be who he is!! Didn't you see him?"

She blinked and tilted her head slightly.

"Somebody has to stop him! Somebody has to stop all these people from yelling! Stop them from breaking the innocence inside of me!"

Inside of me? I didn't mean me, did I?

A peaceful voice came: Look into the mirror that is where you will find yourself. The mirror is a gift. See your reflection and don't judge.

Mirror? I wondered.

I was feeling afraid and I was trying to help this poor little boy. What does that have to do with a mirror?

* * *

I didn't feel safe. It felt like my head was stuck in a tube, like all of my experience was funneling through it.

Wait, that's it! I thought. That's what happens when you are caught in a single aspect experience, everything funnels through just this one thing. I remember telling Soni this.

"Roo," I said. "I think I am having an experience where I'm coming through just a part of me."

Part of me wasn't feeling very sure though, thinking maybe I don't really understand.

Then I saw an image before me. It was of a crystalline sphere. I was standing in the middle with twelve smaller colored spheres arranged around me, like positions on a clock.

I could see that up above and slightly to the left, at about one o'clock, was the part I was funneling through. The sphere was dark, and kept shifting colors.

I heard a voice say: Feel what's inside the sphere, speak to it, it's all you.

I took a deep breath and tuned into the dark sphere. 'I don't feel confident,' it said.

'I'm sorry. What happened that makes you feel this way?' I asked the dark sphere.

'Every time I try to do something, somebody stops me and tells me I'm wrong,' it replied.

'Oh.'

'I don't even feel like trying anymore,' it said. 'Maybe it doesn't matter, I don't know.'

I started feeling gentleness toward this part of me.

'Maybe together we can try, we can keep sharing with each other. I'll share how I feel and leave room for you to play. I would like that,' I said.

'Maybe I would like that, too,' replied the sphere.

It felt like the part of me in the sphere smiled just then. It felt peaceful inside.

Then I flashed over to a swirling orange sphere below on my right. It was at seven o'clock.

There was a lot of fear inside it and I could hear yelling.

'What's happening in there?' I asked the orange sphere.

'You know!' it said. 'You always know. There you go again, yelling at me for this, yelling at me for that. Stand up straight, act tough, don't play with the other kids.... be a man already!'

I felt a bit shocked. The other sphere seemed easier to talk to.

'I'm sorry....' I began saying to the sphere.

'You're not sorry. You're never sorry. You only want to hurt me!'

I paused. 'Maybe you're right. Maybe I haven't let you play. Maybe I do expect you to be something you're not. I'm scared you know. I'm scared you'll get us in trouble. And I'm also sorry,' I said to the swirling sphere.

'Yeah, yeah, I've heard it before. You want to talk to me now, but wait 'til I do something that makes you afraid and you'll be all over my case!' replied the sphere.

I took a moment to feel inside the sphere. I wanted to make room for this part. I didn't want to give up this time.

'I am afraid of how powerful you are,' I said.

'Me? Powerful?' replied the sphere.

'Yes, you are powerful. You aren't afraid to shake things up if it's part of your path.' I started to laugh. 'You sure have created a lot of crazy situations.'

'Yeah, I do...I guess you're right. You mean you like that about me?' it asked, the wall beginning to drop.

'Yes, I love that about you...and it scares me to think that I'm like that!'

'You're like that, too?' it asked.

'Of course I am...I'm you!'

With that my heart filled up with love and compassion. I stopped seeing this part of me as separate. I wanted to give it a hug.

'I love you,' I said feeling emotional. 'Let's keep talking okay?'

'Okay. I love you, too,' it replied.

* * *

I took some time for myself, just loving these parts of me and making more space for them inside.

After a while, I looked up and saw Roo sitting there next to me. It made me smile to see her and I gave her a hug.

"Roo, I had the most amazing experience!" I began. "I learned so much. Like earlier when that guy was yelling, I could hear yelling inside of me. I was standing there over my magical child telling him 'nobody wants what you've got, so go sell it somewhere else'...I can see that now!"

She gave me a kiss and held my hand.

I continued: "There's room for all of me in here. We are all one!"

Chapter 7
Jacard

It was evening time and I was soaking in a hot bath. All this emotional work was exhausting. I could hear Roo downstairs, playing and laughing with the pixies and fairies. As much as I wanted to join her, right now I needed to relax.

I spoke quietly to my spheres: "We can play in a little while. I love you."

Just then Roo popped up the stairs and into the bathroom. "Hi water baby! Don't forget to make a wish for your dog...it's not too late!" She kissed my nose with her moist lips and flew away.

A dog? I asked aloud. What's this about a dog?

The part in the orange sphere started talking. 'I've always wanted a dog! Please can you make another wish?'

'Um, well.... okay...I guess.'

'You guess? No, please don't guess, say yes!' it replied adamantly.

'Okay. I'm sorry. Universe, please send a dog to me, if it's part of my path.'

'No, you have to say how much you want it!' said the orange sphere.

I closed my eyes and tuned into the feeling inside that part of me. 'Please bring me a dog for a friend. I want one more than anything! Please I will take good care of him and love him with all my heart!'

Wow! I didn't know that I had *that* inside me!

The orange sphere felt peaceful again and I took a little nap in the tub.

* * *

When I awoke in the morning, I heard a noise outside. It sounded like a growling of some kind. I jumped up, threw on a pair of sweats and ran out the door.

The noise stopped.

I looked around the yard but saw nothing. Figuring that I was just hearing things, I went back inside.

Then I heard a bark and went back outside.

The noise stopped again.

I walked back into the house, through the kitchen and into the living room and there was Roo playing with the dog from the beach!

"What's he doing here?" I asked, feeling afraid.

"Meet Jacard," said Roo. "I love how you make your wishes come true, puppy love!" She smiled at me.

Jacard? My wish? Oh no.

My orange sphere spoke up: 'Please can we play with him? Please?!'

'Oh...um...okay,' I replied.

'Yeah! Let's go!' I heard the orange sphere say and then found myself running over to play with the dog.

I found a ball and threw it for him to catch. I tried to have fun and play with him, but I was too nervous. "I'm scared," I said to Roo.

Jacard came over and licked me. He lay down next to me, curled up, and put his head on my lap. I saw the deep knowing in his eyes.

Roo came over to curl up, too. She wrapped herself around me and looked at Jacard.

"He's lucky," she said.

"Why do you say that?" I asked.

Her eyes twinkled. "He's got you.... and me," she said.

* * *

My sphere at one o'clock, started to feel scared. 'What is it?' I asked. 'What has you feeling scared?'

'I don't know how to play with a pet. I'm not capable,' it replied.

'Sure you are,' I said. 'Whatever we don't know, we can learn it together.'

'I'll need to ask if it's okay,' replied the sphere.

'Ask who?'

'A grown up,' it said.

Hmm, this part of me still feels like it has to ask someone else for truth. It doesn't trust the knowledge on the inside. I saw another flash and saw my crystalline sphere. I could see that the sphere at one o'clock was disconnected from its higher source.

How do I reconnect it? I wondered.

AQ popped up in front of me. "Hello sir. Were you looking for another upgrade," he said with a giggle.

"AQ! You're just in time. Yes I need help reconnecting the dark sphere," I said pointing to the sphere at the one o'clock spot.

"Okay, connect in with this sphere and remember back to when you were young, prior to when this sphere got squashed," said AQ.

"Alright," I replied.

"Now, what was this sphere's purpose?"

"It was meant to bring in a higher vision of the world and a knowing of how everything works," I said aloud.

As I remembered my purpose and felt the knowing, energy rushed through me.

"Great! Now, close your eyes!" he said giggling again. "We'll take it from here."

* * *

When I opened my eyes again, everything looked clear. I didn't feel blocks inside me anymore. I could feel a knowing, that wasn't there before.

"Roo, this is exciting. I think I'm fixed!" I said aloud.

She laughed at that thought.

Looking over at Jacard, I said: "Hi there fella. Welcome home!"

I stroked his fur gently and allowed all my parts to experience what it feels like to love a dog. My heart felt warm and pure.

And then I stroked Roo's hair tenderly to allow my parts to experience what it feels like to love a Roo.

"I love you," I said to her. "You are my wish come true."

Chapter 8
The Time Of My Heart

Soni and Raji's baby had just been born and they invited us over for a 'Welcome to the World' celebration.

"Roo, what do you think about us having a family?" I asked while we were getting ready.

I was feeling a lot more peaceful since we reconnected my parts and I realized that having a family was one of the other things that I'd always wanted.

Roo was quiet and just listened.

"You know, it took me forever to find you," I teased. "And I had given up on my dream to have a child."

I looked into her eyes, they were swirling and drawing me in closer.

"I want to have a child together, Roo. I want to get you pregnant." I felt my skin flush, this passion reawakened inside of me.

"You don't have to answer now, it's okay, take all the time you need," I said unsure what her thoughts were.

She turned her head and gazed into my eyes. Her beautiful pools blinked once, then blinked again...I rarely saw her do that. Light emitted from her skin, causing goose bumps all over me. The air began to change. A slight wind blew as we sat in our bedroom.

She blinked once more, her eyes now the color of lightning.

The wind picked up and began swirling around her, she raised her arms in the air and looked upward. My body drew in close to her and I wrapped my legs around her. I reached out to touch her hands, instead my fingers slid down her sides, making me shiver.

She returned her stare to me, her eyes now soft wispy clouds. Her energy drew me to her, I fell into her eyes, warmth rushing over my body.

I felt a surge of electricity come in from above.

When I looked up, I saw a bright ball of energy slowly merging in with Roo. She held my stare and took a deep breath. The energy ball completely merged with her energy, melting me. I felt tingles in my hands and feet, then it ran up through my legs into my pelvis.

I took a breath, a deep inhale. I had never experienced anything like this before. Energy continued surging through me as I held her in my arms. She was radiating now, pure pink light surrounding her. Her skin glowed.... literally... from the energy ball.

She smiled and blinked her eyes.

Slowly, she said: "Yes, I'd love to have our child."

* * *

We showed up to Soni and Raji's a bit later than expected, however no one seemed to notice.

"Hey brother!" said Soni. Then he turned to Roo. "You are absolutely glowing, girl...what's your secret?"

I pulled her closer. We both said: "We're having a baby!"

"Come inside, come inside..." He ushered us in. "Raji, guess what, they're having a baby!"

"Oh my gosh, congratulations!" said Raji, holding their new baby. We all did a group hug.

"We are so happy for you both. Congratulations!" said Soni.

Soni was right, Roo is glowing. She's absolutely radiant!

Chapter 9
Eila-roo And Guess Who

Everyone went out to the back yard for a late lunch. Raji was quietly nursing the new baby in a rocking chair on the patio.

"She's so good," said Soni. "This girl sleeps like a lamb."

"Aw, that's nice. She's adorable," I commented. "Hey, what's her name?"

Raji piped up: "Eila-roo!"

Roo smiled and blinked once. Her body glowing with white light.

"Yea, we named her after aunty Roo," Soni said with a laugh, then ran inside to grab a couple drinks.

Raji put the baby down for a nap and sat down outside with us. "How far along are you?" she asked Roo.

"He will be born in two months."

Soni and Raji both turned suddenly in shock. "Really?" said Soni. "You don't look more than…." He looked at Roo's belly. When we arrived, her little belly was barely a bump. Now it was barely held in by her tiny shirt. "Oh," he said, finding something else to do.

* * *

We were all sitting on the grass after lunch. Eila was up from her nap now and Soni was holding her in his arms, telling her stories. She seemed mesmerized by him.

Raji was telling Roo all about her pregnancy. "Girl, it was hard near the end. I was getting bigger and bigger...I couldn't even tie my shoes!" she said with a snort.

I turned toward Soni. He had a puzzled look on his face.

"What is it?" I asked.

"Brother, do you hear that sound?"

I listened to the noises around me. "Which sound, Soni?"

"Like talking," he said turning a bit pale.

"Oh, are you hearing a voice again?" I asked, remembering his ability to channel other worldly beings.

He paused. "Well, something like that, I guess."

I tried to tune in to what he was hearing but I didn't pick up on anything.

"Brother, it sounds like Eila-roo," he said, the words barely making their way out.

"Oh, neat! You can hear Eila talking just like in your dream!"

"It sounds like she's talking to.... to...to..." Soni tried to spit it out.

"To who?" I asked.

"To your baby," he said finally.

Oh.

* * *

"Soni, let's take a walk, okay?" I suggested.

Soni handed Eila to Raji and followed me out the gate.

After a while, I asked: "What's going on, brother?"

"I don't know what's happening to me. I'm not sure why I'm hearing things. Maybe something is wrong with me," Soni replied.

I saw a flash just then. It was a picture of Soni inside his crystalline sphere. I could see that one of his smaller spheres was afraid.

"Soni, can you share what you're feeling? Breathe and feel inside of you," I said.

He took a moment to center. "I feel afraid, afraid of the magical part of me." He paused.

I remained silent, leaving space for his truth, for his feelings.

"I really just don't know why I'm so scared. Where is the fear coming from?" he asked.

I looked at his spheres once more. "Picture your twelve smaller spheres as positions on the clock. The sphere that's in the five o'clock position is separated from the rest of you. That's your magical part. Now, breathe and tune into that part, what does it have to say?"

Soni took a deep cleansing breath. I could see his energy clear up, the static subsiding. "I had a bad experience when I was young. My mother was changing me into a clean diaper.... and I started to float up off the table. I began communicating to her telepathically and she could hear me!" he said taking another breath. "She got so freaked out that she grabbed me from the air and held me down on the table. She was chanting something, it sounded like she was praying for the gods to cure me."

He looked up at me, eyes tearing. "Man, that was a sight..." He reached over and hugged me. There was a sense of relief about him, that he finally revealed and released this hidden pain.

I watched as his sphere connected back up to the rest of him.

Wow! I thought. That was beautiful.

As we walked back to the house, I asked: "Hey, brother, so what were those two talking about anyway?"

We both laughed.

Chapter 10

Room For Baby

It was evening time, when Roo and I returned home. This seemed like the longest day! I was starting to feel like I needed to slow down.

"Roo, I just want to hold you. Would you come lay down with me?" I asked kissing her hand.

She followed me upstairs and into our bedroom. The window was still open from earlier, there was a nice breeze blowing in.

I lay down on the bed and Roo curled up next to me. She felt so nice. Her skin was warm and it smelt like flowers. For the first time, I reached down to feel her growing belly. Energy ran through my fingers, up through my hand and arm.

"Wow! Roo your belly! It's getting so round...and you feel amazing!" It made me want to hold her more. I leaned over and kissed her tummy. Electricity sparked in the air.

This little guy was pretty special, I could tell already.

I saw a picture flash before me. It was of our baby. He was communicating with me, sharing his purpose and his name.

"His name is Ashrial," I said aloud. "He will be born in two months, much sooner than Earth babies. His purpose is to reawaken the magical children of the planet."

Ashrial, I thought. Isn't that the being that spoke to Soni before our mountain trip?

"Welcome Ashrial," said Roo to her belly.

I returned my focus to her. She was looking like an angel, love flowing from her, light glowing from her skin. My heart was melting inside.

I fell asleep in her arms.

* * *

When I awoke, it was morning. Roo was just getting out of the shower. Her fresh round body practically shining.

"Come back to bed, Roo. Let me hold you more.... please." I felt like I was craving her, it had never felt this way before.

She curled up in bed and gave me a long kiss. My pulse shot up and caused me to gasp for a breath of air.

"Roo, I am so attracted to you. Every thing you do, everything you are...it's all driving me crazy." I felt flushed by her presence. "I need to be near you."

She smiled and pulled in closer. Her eyes now staring into mine, drawing me in. The wind picked up and blew the wind chimes outside the window. Flashes of light shot into the room. She wrapped herself around me in an embrace...I felt like I was becoming one with her spirit.

"Let go," she whispered.

I let everything go....

The room started spinning and I merged in with her, I felt Ashrial next to me, felt his heart beating...I felt the warmth of her body...and just melted in.

"Stay with me...in oneness we shall be..." she whispered in my ear. Shivers ran through my body.

I let go a bit more and joined with her spirit. I could feel a celebration inside, it called me to be near and opened my heart in a way I'd never felt. I felt one with everything.

One with Roo.

The wind whipped up one last time and we were gone.

Chapter 11

Arianon

Roo and I dropped down into a field of grass and flowers. Just up ahead was the little girl that we'd seen so many times before. She was sitting on the grass playing, many creatures and mystical friends around her.

I heard a voice say: Look inside yourself. You are one.

I thought for a moment and then approached the girl. 'May I sit down?' I transmitted.

She nodded.

'You have a gift to bring,' I began. 'Do you remember?'

She nodded again.

'Show me,' I transmitted.

The little girl got up and walked over to her parents, she held their hands and raised their vibration. Then her parents suddenly lit up like stars and lifted off the ground. They started spinning in the air, whirling faster and faster until finally their magical child parts popped up and reconnected with the rest of them. I watched as their spheres were instantly repaired to near perfection. Slowly they were placed back on the earth again, their eyes glowing, still holding her hands. They looked at me and then back down to their daughter.

As I started to leave, I heard them transmit 'Thank you.'

'You're welcome,' I replied. Then we popped back home.

* * *

"She was some kid," I remarked. "I hope Ashrial is like her."

Roo looked at me and smiled. "You are amazing," she said.

I blushed slightly, still getting used to the magical me.

"So are you," I replied.

"What was that?" I asked suddenly feeling a kick.

"Hi Ashrial," said Roo.

"You mean that was him? How did I feel that?" I asked.

'We are all one,' she transmitted.

Chapter 12
Why, I Knew That

The sun was shining outside. Roo was lying on the grass, soaking in the warm rays.

I kept hearing Ashrial. He was sending more information about who he is and his unique purpose on the planet. I was getting excited thinking that he was going to be here soon.

Roo's little belly wasn't little anymore. She looked like she was six months pregnant, so round and cute. And she just glowed from every part of her.

In my mind, the thought stirred about writing a book with Roo...I think it was being downloaded as I sat there under the tree.

We had a bit of savings left, probably just enough for our next adventure, I thought to myself.

Just then, a little girl sat down next to me. I was surprised at first and then I recognized her. It was the girl from the field.

'I am Arianon,' she transmitted.

'Arianon,' I responded. 'How are you?'

She looked into my eyes intently, as if she was looking for something.

'Don't you remember me?' she asked telepathically.

'Yes? I think so.' I was now questioning what she meant.

Suddenly everything swirled and we slipped into a different reality. The air around me was moist and there was moss on the ground. She sat down by a patch of flowers and began humming.

My head started to spin. I remember that tune, I said to myself. I remember this place.

"Princess!" I yelled aloud.

She smiled and magically the flowers that she had been playing with became a crown. Her dress turned into vines, flowers, leaves and dewdrops.

"It's you," I said softly.

She nodded her head.

I began to remember. When I was small I would go play in the woods. I imagined lots of things, there were friends and animals. We always had a lot of fun. My imagination went wild and I loved it.

Once this vision came to me of a little girl, she was beautiful with dark eyes and soft hair. She came to play with me everyday. We had so many adventures.

But I could only see her when I was alone in the woods.

I guess part of me thought she was made up. Now I was seeing that she was real. She'd been real the whole time.

'How did you stay small?' I asked telepathically.

'Silly,' she replied. 'It's magic!'

'Why, I knew that!' I transmitted. 'It's magic!'

* * *

From that day on, Arianon popped by our house and brought magical adventure. Roo and I introduced her to our pixie friends and to Sireal, the gnome. She enlisted Jacard to be the doggie bus for fairies and wrapped ribbons around him.

I let that playful part of me out for good and invited my imagination to wake back up!

One day when Arianon was there, playing in the trees, the wind started to shift, suddenly the three of us were whisked away.

When we popped up, we were all at Soni's place.

What are we doing here? I wondered.

Soni and Raji walked out and both said telepathically: 'What took you so long?'

Huh? I thought.

Soni ushered us inside where their daughter, Eila-roo was floating around the room. "She just learned how to fly upside down...and we couldn't wait to show you!" said Soni.

Roo and I looked at each other and burst out laughing.

"Isn't it great that we're all one!"

Part III
Simply Enlightened

Contents

Chapter 1
Right Of Passage

It was about a month away from Ashrial's birth. Roo was round in the middle. She radiated more than ever, something I didn't even think was possible. She buzzed around like a fairy, completely alive.

My dreams were becoming wild. I was walking through them consciously, fully aware of what was happening and why. And they were drifting over more and more into my awake time.

Last night I had a dream that seemed to allow me into a different world.

There was an older woman standing by the edge of a forest waiting for me. She was holding a long wooden staff. Her energy connected all the way down through the earth and up to the heavens, even connected to each and every living thing around her.

It gave me chills.

"Aiyana?" I asked, though already knowing.

She nodded then motioned for me to follow her.

We walked into the woods together. Her bare feet, quiet as silence on the ground. She led me deep within the trees where there was a circle of rocks.

She motioned for me to stand in the center. Out of a sack she pulled some stones and a feather. She held them in her hand and raised her arms in the air, as if calling in forces from above.

This strange energy began to circle me, spiraling upward. Then a voice echoed in the air, "Dancing wolf you are gifted, precious to the Earth and her people...rise and carry them to where they are pure again...let the strength of your ancestors hold you, allowing true power to rule...grateful warrior, it is time to end the war."

I could feel something enter my body, something strong. It was an energy I hadn't experienced before. I allowed it to run through me, trusting in it.

When it was complete, the circling energy was gone. I looked down and there was a marking on my chest. It was of a wolf!

"Aiyana, what does this mean?" I asked, surprised.

She handed me a small stone, then lit a mugwort and sage stick purifying me in a smoky cloud.

Without a word, she led me out of the forest.

* * *

When I woke in the morning, a slightly dazed feeling washed over me. I felt dizzy in the head, yet my energy was higher than ever. I looked over to see if Roo was still sleeping and she wasn't there. Lately she all but stopped needing to sleep. That was something I couldn't even conceive of at the moment.

I stumbled downstairs to find Sireal building a nest for the baby in the living room, using Jacard, the dog, as a ladder.

I needed to get out of here.

Was everyone else ready but me? I felt like I was falling behind. Am I the one that gets left behind? I thought. What does Roo need with a bumbling human anyway?

* * *

I found myself walking out the door and down the road, unsure where I was headed. Unsure why I was leaving. Feeling scared out of my mind.

Maybe I'll go see Soni, I thought. He usually understands things.

So, off I went to Soni's place. He was about thirty minutes walk from here, that would give me plenty of time to think.

I knocked on the front door, no answer. I walked around back, no sign of anyone.

I started to slump, feeling a bit hopeless and useless. Not a good combination.

Just then Soni walked up. "Hey brother, what's going on?" He gave me a hug. "Uh oh, you don't feel so good," he said, noticing my droopy energy.

"I think I should give up, Soni. Maybe I should just let Roo go to have the baby. She doesn't need me," I said practically sobbing.

"Come inside for a minute. I'll let Raji know we're going out for a while." I followed him inside the house.

Eila-roo was floating around, playing with a little creature I'd not seen before.

Raji said: "Hey, good to see you, brother. You know Eila has been showing us how to breathe underwater...it's amazing!"

"Is everyone ready but me?!!!" I yelled, storming out of the house.

I could hear Soni calling for me as I ran down the street and kept right on running.

I need to be alone, I thought.

* * *

There I was sprawled out over a big flat rock at my secret spot when Soni showed up.

"Brother?" he began slowly.

"Yes," I said, barely audible.

"Mind if I come over there?"

"Whatever..." I replied.

I could hear the water splash as Soni hopped from rock to rock. Soon he was sitting next to me.

We let the silence sit between us for a long while. It was peaceful. I felt safer with him there.

"Brother, I love you. I'm sorry that you're hurting like this." Soni's eyes teared up. "I'm scared too sometimes, brother. Nobody's above it."

I started crying again.

I sat up and gave Soni a hug, gripping him for life. "Brother, I'm so alone! I don't know what to do. I just don't know what to do!" I yelled.

We held each other, both of us crying, releasing all our held pain.

"We can only take it one step at a time," Soni said at last. "Will you keep taking them with me, brother? One at a time?"

I looked into his dark eyes. They seemed so soft today. I'd never seen him like this.

"Okay, one at a time," I said still sobbing. "Not without you though, we can't do it alone anymore."

* * *

Soni and I spent the rest of the day at the spot. We began to envision the world in a new way. We had lots of ideas and now it was time to take them back home, to share them with others.

Soni stopped by his house to pick up Raji and Eila-roo. Together we drove to my house. When we arrived Roo was outside, a full picnic dinner set out on the table.

"Roo, how did you know?" I asked, surprised.

She just smiled and blinked. The colors in the evening sky changed.

I looked into her eyes and gave her a hug. "Roo, I love you!"

During dinner, Soni and I shared our vision. "We see that it's time to come together," Soni began. "Anyone that's ready will find us or we'll find them, a circle will be created."

"And we need to start here first. We will work together to build a house here for Soni, Raji and Eila," I said, eyes wide with excitement. "We will create space for us, for Ashrial, for Eila and all the other beings coming into an enlightened awareness. It will be a place of magic and light, all beings welcome!"

Eila let out a shriek.

Soni started laughing. "She just said how happy she is. She has been waiting to come here!"

"The passage way is open, come on in!" I said with a smile.

Chapter 2
Creation And Birth

"Guess what?" Soni said over the phone. "This guy I haven't talked to in years, just called. He has been looking for other people like him. He wants to start a sacred circle to bring people together!" Soni paused. "He's coming here, he wants to help us build a center!"

"What? Are you serious? Just like that?" I was shocked and elated.

"Yes. He'll be here in two weeks," Soni said. "Hey, can he stay with you?"

"Of course. We'll work something out. Soni, I'm so happy!"

After our goodbyes, I hung up the phone.

Now the flow is starting and everything is coming together. I've only experienced being alone in all my creations.

There was a pang inside of me. I stopped what I was doing and took a deep breath.

I feel scared. I don't know how to be part of the big energy that I feel. Roo is flying already, what about me?

I took another deep breath.

Oh yeah, one step at a time.

* * *

Soni and I invited some people to come over to my place. It was time for networking, calling in our resources.

At seven o'clock people started showing up. Seranga came bringing two friends of hers. Soni and Raji brought Solana, their neighbor with the hot tub, plus three other people that Soni knew.

Wow, I thought. I didn't know so many people would come.

We all went to sit around the big fire pit in the back yard. Soni began sharing our vision. "We are being called to create a sacred circle for all those who are ready. Each of you is here because you felt it in your heart, the idea resonated in you."

"Our purpose is simple: to bring those beings together that want more light, more love, more play, more truth in their lives," I added.

"We want to wake up the magical child inside each of us and give them a place to be," said Soni. "I am ready for that. And we can do it, one step at a time." Soni smiled, then looked up. My friends Marty and Jon had just arrived.

"Over here," we called in unison. They introduced themselves to the rest of the group.

Laughter and chatter filled the evening air as people shared their visions with each other around the warm fire.

Just then, there was a pop and Arianon suddenly appeared. "Hello," she said, giggling. "I am ready!"

People around the fire circle turned to see what just happened. Then, Soni said with a laugh: "All beings are welcome, no matter where they come from."

Jacard ran over and licked Soni's face, everyone began chuckling.

* * *

Later, after everyone left, Roo and I sat in our room talking.

"Roo, it's amazing how everyone is coming together. I've never experienced this before, not in all my life."

She smiled at me and kissed my nose.

"It's like all the energy is already out there and you just need to match your steps to it," I said. "Whatever it is that you are feeling in the moment."

I was silent for a while. Roo just held me and toozled my hair.

"You know Roo, I've been feeling so separate from you, I mean with the baby coming and all," I began. "You're pregnant, you're growing a child inside of you. In fact, you're flying around the house with tons of energy, barely sleeping."

I paused before continuing.

"I feel left out of the whole thing," I said, tears filled my eyes and my throat felt choked up.

"Baby snuggly bear, it's our pregnancy, our child, and he is in our bodies." She kissed me, sending energy through my body.

"What do you mean, Roo? I'm not carrying Ashrial. Am I?" I asked.

"Close your eyes, lovey-bean," she said gently.

I closed my eyes and instantly I saw how we created Ashrial. It was with both our bodies! It required both our creation centers to be activated. We are both connected to him.

"Does that mean I can fly, too?" I asked, opening my eyes.

Roo smiled and with a blink, I lifted off the bed and into the air.

Chapter 3
Wake Up The Spring

It was a sunny day and Soni called to invite us for a hike. "Hey brother, we're taking Eila-roo for her first hike on the mountain. Do you want to go?"

"Sure, we'd love to. Roo and I will pack some snacks and meet you there," I said hanging up.

I turned around and Roo was standing there with our pack in hand, all ready to go. I had to smile, she could be so cute.

We met up with Soni, Raji and Eila at the base parking lot and headed up the trail. Soni was leading the way.

About three miles up, he made a turn to the left and veered of the standard path. Soni led us through a garden of flowers and rocks, around trees and berry bushes, finally stopping at a clearing.

"Do you hear that?" he asked.

We all listened.

"Water!" said Raji.

Soni led us over to the base of a beautiful waterfall with a large pool of water under it.

"How did you know?" she asked.

"Magic," he replied laughing.

* * *

Raji and Roo hopped in first. They held Eila and danced her around under the falls. Eila giggled and shrieked.

Soni and I were watching them rather satisfactorily. "I'm so glad we came up here, brother," he said at last.

"Me, too," I replied. "You know this is exactly what's missing at the house."

"What?" asked Soni.

"The natural flow of water. We have plenty in the woods, but nothing on the property." I thought for a moment. "What we need is a pool of natural water."

"That's true. It works wonders for healing," said Soni.

"Yes and it's great for learning to breathe under water!" I said laughing.

With that, the two of us left our clothes and ran to jump into the water. "I'll beat you there!" called Soni over his shoulder.

I popped over there instead and beat him by a minute.

"Hey, brother, that's not fair. When are you going to show me that trick?" Soni pouted.

"It's magic," I replied, dunking myself fully under the water.

Maybe it's time to learn to breathe under water, I thought to myself.

* * *

Later on, back at the house, we all sat around the fire. Raji had nursed Eila to sleep and she was nestled in her arms. Soni and I shared our idea aloud.

"We're missing water here on the land," Soni began.

"Yea, let's use some magic and wake it back up again. Get the water flowing," I said.

Just then, I felt Ashrial moving inside. I turned around and held Roo's belly.

"Ashrial is almost here, we need a beautiful natural place for him to be born. Roo and I could birth him right in the water!" I said, rubbing her tummy. She felt so sweet, so peaceful. I could really feel him now. His presence was around us, in every way.

Roo smiled and nodded approvingly. "I love you, spring bunny!" she said.

"I love you, too and I can't wait to have our baby together. To hold him in our arms and to watch him learn to fly!" I paused. "Maybe he can show me a few things." I smiled at Roo and blinked once, changing the lighting outside.

* * *

The next day we planned to get together again and have a 'wake up the spring' party. And I couldn't wait. It would feel so good to have water flowing on our land.

Roo and I spent some time together during the day going slow and holding each other. She was curled up on our bed, looking very pregnant, her eyes closed.

"Roo," I said caressing her warm skin. "How's Ashrial doing in there?"

She blinked her eyes.

I could feel inside of her body again. I could feel Ashrial. Pleasant shivers ran through me.

Just then I saw Ashrial's body move across her belly, light glowing around him.

"He's coming!" I said suddenly.

Roo looked into my eyes and smiled.

* * *

Soni and the gang showed up around four o'clock, all of them smiling from ear to ear. Shortly after, Elu walked down the road and up to the house.

"Hey, Elu! Thanks for being here!" I said giving him a big hug.

"I wouldn't miss it, brother. The Earth has been calling me, too," he replied.

I walked them over to the spot where the land was asking for help.

"Are you ready?" I asked.

Everyone nodded. Jacard barked.

We placed our hands on the ground and sent light and love into it. Energy swirled around us and the earth started to shift. Animals came out of the woods to join us. Pixies, fairies and gnomes popped in from nowhere and helped as well.

The wind picked up and blew hard against us. We focused more energy into the earth. It began to crack open and move.

Within minutes there was not only a spring but also a medium size pool of water right there in that spot! It was deep and steam was floating from the top. Big boulders erupted from the earth surrounding the pool, even some plants popped out of the ground, making it look like it had been there for years.

"Oh my gosh, I'm so grateful. I'm so happy!" I said, crying. Everyone was hugging one another and crying in a dance around the pool.

I looked up. "Thank you to everyone who came here today!"

That's when I saw them. It was Arianon and her parents. They must have arrived while we were working.

I smiled at them and waved. "Thank you for coming."

* * *

Soni cleared his throat. "Attention! May I have everyone's attention, please," he said.

I turned around.

What was this? I wondered.

"We got an offer on the house today and we accepted." He smiled wide. "We'll be moving here next week."

"That's great!" I said and howled in the air like a wolf.

Everything is coming together!

Chapter 4
Coming Together

Soni's friend from out of town was coming in today. He is the one that wants to help create a center and a sacred circle. Things were looking up.

With help from the fairies and Sireal, we set up the living room as a temporary guest room. We hung a curtain in the doorway for privacy and set up the fold out bed. The pixies decorated it with flowers.

In the early afternoon, Soni drove up with his friend. They got out and walked toward the house.

"Hey brother," I heard Soni call from outside.

Roo and I walked out to greet them.

"Hey Soni." We gave him a hug.

"This is the friend I've been telling you about. His name is Martin," said Soni.

Jacard ran up and licked him. "Nice to meet you," said Martin, shaking our hands and petting Jacard.

"Come on inside, I'll show you where to put your things," I said leading him through the door and into the living room.

* * *

Martin met up with us outside. He was tall. This was the first time I really noticed him. Tall with long dark hair. He had a familiar look to him, yet his energy was like no one I'd ever known.

"Hey Martin, I'm going to catch you later, huh? We have an appointment with the sales agent," said Soni, giving him a hug.

"Good to see you again, Soni-mon," replied Martin.

With that Soni was gone.

I stood there looking at Martin, his dark eyes appeared to see right through me.

"I'm ready, mon," said Martin without shifting his gaze.

"Ready?" I asked.

"Let's get this healing started. I was told about who you are and what you can do for me," replied Martin.

Just then, as if on queue, AQ popped up. "Gartanimo, good to see you," said AQ to Martin.

Huh? Who's Gartanimo?

"Gartanimo is Martin, they are one in the same," replied AQ to my silent question.

Oh. So we already know him then.

"Yes," replied Roo aloud to my thoughts.

That's why he seems so familiar, I thought to myself.

"Right," replied Gartanimo, confirming my thoughts.

"Hey, can everyone hear me?" I asked aloud.

'Yes,' they all replied without words.

* * *

"Gartanimo, we need to start repairs on your sphere and replace some older wiring," said AQ. "When you are ready, please close your eyes and we'll take it from here."

And with that, Gartanimo was out like a light. We helped his already resting body to lie down on the grass.

"He will need about three days to integrate all these changes," AQ said to me. "Make sure he gets plenty of rest."

"Okay, will do," I replied. With another pop, AQ was gone again.

* * *

Later in the day Gartanimo, who was now up from his sphere work, sat on the ground by our newly created pool. I watched him as he meditated, white light energy flowed down through the top of his head on down the rest of his body. He was emitting a beautiful pink energy. I could hear him quietly toning.

The meditation experience that he was having began transferring over to my body and I felt cozy inside, even soft around my heart.

'Thank you,' I telepathed. Then turned and walked away.

When I walked back in the house, the phone was ringing. "Hello," I said picking up the receiver.

"Brother, I need to talk. I'm coming over okay?" said Soni.

"Sure. I'll see you in a few," I replied.

Something was happening. I could feel Soni's energy and it felt far away from him.

I sat down to meditate under my favorite tree to wait for him.

About fifteen minutes later, Soni walked up and sat down. He let out a long sigh.

"There's a problem, brother. The buyer isn't sure they want to go through with the sale," he said.

"Hmm, I'm sorry, brother," I replied.

Then I saw a flash, it was Roo's face. She was telling me to go get Gartanimo.

"Come on, Soni. Let's go talk to Gartanimo, I mean Martin," I said, getting up.

Gartanimo heard us coming and said to Soni: "Mon, you need to collect all parts of you. Bring 'em home."

Soni's face flushed. "What parts?"

Gartanimo continued: "There is a huge part of you and Raji in that house. All your energy should be with you, not in a building."

"Oh. Okay. I gotta go...I'll see you guys later!" And Soni drove away.

Wow! This guy is amazing! How does he do it?

'It's part of you, too,' Gartanimo transmitted. 'We're all one.'

Chapter 5

The Shift

The third day into Gartanimo's energy sphere upgrades and he was better than ever. He had been sleeping on the ground at night and walking on the earth with his bare feet during the day. It felt like he was at one with everything around him.

I watched him from a distance, unsure if I should approach and disturb him.

* * *

In the early afternoon, Roo and I were just getting back from our walk. We heard this strange sound through the trees. When we arrived at home, we saw Gartanimo in the back yard with about four other people. They were all playing didgeridoos into the earth! Jacard was sitting with them, barking and howling to the music.

I craved to join in..... I wanted what he had. I couldn't believe that I was feeling this way.

I held Roo in my arms and closed my eyes, virtually feeling and experiencing their rhythms. I felt closer to Roo, closer to Ashrial, closer to me!

Just then, Gartanimo called: "Mon, come on. We have an extra didj, must be for you."

Roo looked at me with a warm smile and we hopped over to join them.

We blew healing energy into the earth for more than two hours. Sometimes taking turns to give others a break. Roo sat down in the middle of the circle.

When the energy got really high, she lifted up off the ground.

* * *

The evening came and we all sat around the fire ring talking. It turns out more than half the people there are ready to help us create a center! I had no idea. Gartanimo had such a way about him.

Soni showed up with Raji and Eila and they joined us by the fire. They looked happy. Their energy felt good.

"We brought some of our things, brother," said Soni. "Once we took our energy out of the house.... poof, like magic the buyers set a closing date! It was crazy!"

Raji added: "It was weird, brother, the house felt really empty after that. Who knew."

"Congratulations," I said feeling peaceful. I was glad that they were coming here.

Gartanimo said: "Mon, it sounds like a good time for music!" And he began playing a hand drum. Some of the other people picked up their didgeridoos to accompany him.

Raji grabbed Roo for a dance.

Elu walked out of the shadows and said: "If you are going to dance, soul sister, dance to heal the Earth." He curled the corners of his mouth, then said: "And don't forget to invite me next time you throw a party."

I laughed. "Didn't you get the message? We transmitted it hours ago. What took you so long?"

I ran over to give Elu a hug. "He's coming," I said by his ear.

"I know," he replied.

Chapter 6

Planting Seeds

The morning light was just beginning to creep in through the window. Roo was lying next to me holding Ashrial...

HUH?!

"Roo! When did he get here?!" I asked, completely shocked.

"He landed this morning at 2 a.m.," she said giving me a kiss. "Isn't he precious, lover bee?"

My heart was practically jumping out of my chest. How did this happen? Why didn't I know?

"Uhh...Yes, of course he is, but Roo I didn't know," I said feeling lost.

She smiled at me and then....

I woke up.

* * *

"Roo, I had the craziest dream," I said waking her. "You were holding Ashrial, he just appeared! I'm so glad to still see your round tummy."

She blinked once washing away the dark corners in the room.

I thought about the dream while I was holding her.

"How do you give birth, Roo? Is it different than Earth birth?"

She blinked again and a picture flashed in front of me. I saw Ashrial landing down through her. His energy forming outside of her, then transforming into solid form.

"That's how it happens? It is so much easier! I wonder why everyone doesn't birth this way," I said aloud. Roo giggled.

I gave her a kiss and we went back to bed.

* * *

Around two o'clock Soni and Raji stopped by carrying a small tree. "Hey brother! We felt like our next step was to plant a tree, you know to connect our energy to the earth over here," said Raji.

"Cool, where does it want to go?" I asked.

They walked around the yard for a bit then called me over. "Right here," they said together.

It was the side yard, where the garden is. I thought that was perfect.

"It's an apple tree, so we'll have fresh fruit!" said Raji excitedly.

"I love it, Raji," I replied. "Do you need a shovel?"

Just then Jacard poked out from around the corner. He was carrying Sireal on his back with a small shovel. Sireal hopped down and got to work digging the hole.

Soni started laughing so hard he fell over onto the grass.

* * *

We had finished planting the tree and Soni was putting some boxes into my storage space. I was outside meditating on the grass.

"It's time," said Roo standing by the fresh pool outside.

The hair stood up on the back of my neck.

Time?

I got up and ran over to her side.

"What do we do?" I asked, out of breath.

"Hold my hands, love," replied Roo.

Soni and Raji came out of the house just then and knew right away what was happening. They held hands with each other, making a circle around Roo and I.

Jacard ran over and barked.

The energy began spiraling around all of us. The sky above seemed to open up sending light rays streaming. The once calm wind now shifted picking up leaves that were on the ground and throwing them about.

Gartanimo, who was on the other side of the yard, had walked over to where we stood. "Oh, it's time, mon. Good for you," he said aloud, joining the circle with Soni and Raji.

Roo's breathing changed, it got heavier and more powerful. I shifted to match her breathing. Sheets of rain came pouring down on us and the sky was streaked with lightning bolts.

Light shot out from Roo's eyes. And then from other parts of her body, like her hands and feet. Her skin looked transparent gold with swirling dark lines through it.

She took a deep breath.

Elu walked out of the forest, carrying a sack. He approached us, then placed a feather in Roo's hair. He gave her a kiss and joined the growing circle that surrounded Roo and I.

Roo's little nose wrinkled up as a bumpy formation emerged from the center of her forehead, in the shape of a star. We both took another deep breath.

I heard something above me and looked up to see a group of fairies overhead. I had never seen so many of them before!

Then Sireal popped up out of the ground with a bunch of gnomes, probably ten of them and joined the circle.

Roo and I took another cleansing breath.

Slowly we moved over into the pool...all of us.

AQ popped out of the sky. "Oh, how exciting!" he said.

I watched as Ashrial dropped down through her and into the water with his energy body. Roo and I exhaled, light still swirling around us. Everyone was chanting now and calling in energy. Ashrial moved and darted through the water.

It seemed like we were in another reality!

Arianon suddenly popped in and gave Ashrial a magical kiss, then joined the circle.

Moments later, Ashrial's Earth body had formed and we held him in our arms for the first time. I was crying and holding Roo.

Ashrial blinked and looked into our eyes with a little smile. The light seemed to change in the sky.

Chapter 7

Open Your Eyes

I woke up in the morning, earlier than usual. I had been dreaming a lot, leaving me with a dizzy feeling.

I put Ashrial next to me in the bed holding him close to my heart. His eyes looked like Roo's. They were swirling pools of light, only his had a touch of the sky in them.

'Ashrial,' I telepathed. 'Tell me your secrets.... please.'

I was holding his little hand when he gazed into my eyes and began communicating without words.

He shared more about the book Roo and I will write. It is called 'The Enlightened Way'. We will collaborate with other beings to bring the full knowledge of truth that's available on the planet and further will create a center for all those seeking truth and seeking more of themselves.

He outlined everything in such detail that I felt a bit overwhelmed by it. Then he told me not to worry, just be and everything will come. Ashrial blinked his big swirling eyes and telepathed one more message: 'Everything is already done.'

I smiled at him and drew him closer. He was so small yet wiser than anyone I knew.

* * *

Roo got up from her napping place close to the ceiling and Ashrial flew over to her. He nurses from her breast for nourishment, but not just milk. He drinks in light! That is his main source of sustenance. He is an amazing being.

I walked over and gave her a kiss, holding her in my arms while our little being filled up his body with light. Electric energy shot through me.

Is that what it's like to drink light? I wondered.

* * *

Later in the day, Soni called. He needed some help moving their things into storage and asked if I would help. Of course I agreed.

Roo, Ashrial, Gartanimo and I hopped into the truck to drive to Soni's place. Ashrial blinked and popped us from the driveway to a parking spot right in front of Soni's house.

"Cool ride, mon," said Gartanimo, getting out of the truck. "Can you teach me that one?" he asked Ashrial.

Ashrial just giggled.

We walked inside and met up with Soni. "Hey brother, thanks for coming over. I have most of the things in boxes, we can just carry them out to the truck, okay?" he asked.

Ashrial blinked his big eyes and everything that was in the house was now in the truck! Everything including all of us!

Eila-roo thought this was a kick and let out a shriek.

"Brother, can he drive, too?" asked Soni, jokingly.

Another blink of Ashrial's eyes and all the boxes were gone from the back of the truck.

"Hey where did everything go?" Soni asked getting excited.

I laughed. "Ashrial said the boxes are in storage," I replied to Soni.

'Isn't that where you wanted them?' telepathed Ashrial with a giggle.

Gartanimo started laughing. Soni's jaw dropped.

* * *

A few days later, Gartanimo began sharing some news with me: "Mon, you are going to love this! A few years ago, some friends and I started a non-profit hoping to create a healing center of sorts. Not too much happened right away. Then over time people donated money and we played concerts and things to build up some flow." He walked closer to me, his dark eyes wide with excitement. "Get this! We just checked in on recent donations and there had been a unknown donation for one million dollars!"

"What? That's crazy," I said feeling completely shocked.

"Yeah, I know, mon. It gets better...we want to use the money to create the center here!"

My head started to spin. "Are you serious?" I asked, trying to hold my balance.

"Absolutely! We all agreed!" replied Gartanimo.

I leaned against the counter for support. I couldn't believe this was happening.

* * *

Gartanimo went to call our group together, everyone that was at the sacred circle, plus some other people he knew. He was inviting them over to share the news.

"Roo," I said. "How is this possible? I mean I'm so grateful, but how did it happen?"

Ashrial looked over at me and blinked, casting a pink hue on the walls. Then he telepathed: 'It is all already done.'

This was all great, but I needed to talk to Soni.

* * *

I met up with Soni at the lake. We took a long walk.

"Brother, I hear you. That is a lot of money. But it's fabulous, I wouldn't question it, just enjoy," said Soni.

"I feel like the world is swirling around me, Soni. It doesn't feel good. The energy is flying sky high, I'm just not used to it yet," I replied.

Then, I saw a picture flash in front of me, outlining my purpose and showing the energy of the world.

I heard the words: Everything is energy, including money. Alone it does not make things possible. It is co-creating that makes things happen.

Co-creating? I wondered. What is that?

"Co-creating is when you see everything as one," Soni answered to my nonverbal question. "When there are no lines, when there is no separation."

He gave me a hug. "It's going to be okay, brother. When energy goes high, it can be freaky. Just sit with it, ride it out like a wave."

Chapter 8
Leaving It All Behind

In the early evening, people began showing up. Gartanimo was getting everything ready. He was pulling out instruments, showing our guests around the property, even building a fire in the pit.

I on the other hand, was hiding.

I wasn't really feeling part of the creation. I kept feeling like I was on the receiving end of something, while everyone else was out there creating.

Gartanimo walked over to me with a clever smile. "Hey mon, want to play the didj? You know it'll make you feel better," he said.

"Not right now," I replied.

"Everyone brings a piece of the puzzle, mon. Just let go," said Gartanimo.

Let go, I thought. How could I let go?

"You have everything that you need, let the rest fall away. Don't try. Everything is already done," he continued.

I looked up and stared into his eyes. Something in me started to change. There was a shift.

A piece of the puzzle.... everyone has a piece.

* * *

There was a group of about fifty people gathered out in the yard. People were playing music, laughing and talking. I stood slightly away from any particular crowd. I could feel myself holding back.

"Everyone," said Gartanimo. "Great news. We have a donation to begin the creation of our center." Cheers filled the air.

He continued: "And we finally have a place to build it…right here! Thanks to our new friend and his family." Gartanimo pointed to me, Roo and Ashrial. More cheers.

They didn't have a place until now? It's because of me and the land I have? I didn't know that.

"The Enlightened Way, will birth itself on this sacred ground! People, animals and otherworldly beings will all have a place to come to. It will be a place of creation and a healing space for those who are ready to leave the old ways behind," said Gartanimo. Jacard ran over and started barking happily.

"Truly, I want to say thank you mon, for everything you've done," he said looking straight into my eyes.

"The Enlightened Way?" I asked him.

"Yes, it's the name we received from spirit when we started our non-profit," replied Gartanimo.

I stood there kind of blank and then a small smile crept its way across my face.

The center will be The Enlightened Way? I thought to myself. That's funny! That is really funny! I began to laugh out loud. Laughing at how ridiculous it was, how upset I'd been. The people around me started laughing, too. I'm not sure why, maybe it was infectious. Either way, laughter filled the night air, warming my heart.

"You're welcome," I said finally. "And thank you as well."

We are all one, I said to myself.

I am finally beginning to understand my purpose!

* * *

Though I felt more relief, something inside me was still troubled and it was screaming to get out. I went for a walk in the woods hoping for a release. Praying for wisdom.

A light rain fell, bringing peace to my spirit.

As I walked I asked for answers. Spirit please help me. This feels big and I don't know what it is or what to do, I said aloud.

The wind blew slightly and I heard a voice: "You cannot ride out this wave."

The voice paused for a moment before continuing.

"Everything connects to you, to your power center. So, stop creating, just let it all fall away. Focus inward instead. Let the sphere within you rebalance as you grow strong and whole again."

I sat down in the middle of the woods, in the middle of the rain, and let go.

Chapter 9

Through The Open Door

It was late when I returned from my walk. I went upstairs and curled up with Roo and Ashrial.

"You still awake, Roo?" I asked quietly.

She turned and looked at me, blinking her eyes once adjusting the brightness of the moon. Then she lifted up Ashrial and gently placed him in my arms.

I held him close to me and began crying again, sobbing for my own lost childhood, for the loss of years without my magical parts.

'I'm ready,' I telepathed. 'I don't want to struggle to be magical anymore!'

Ashrial smiled and giggled. 'You are done.'

'What do you mean?' I transmitted to him.

'You came here this lifetime to complete certain things and you did. Now you get to release the old ways and allow your full being to merge into your body. It's time for magic,' he telepathed.

'Good, I'm ready for that!' I laughed. 'And it's about time!'

* * *

AQ popped in just then and began communicating with Ashrial telepathically. 'Lord Ashrial, good to see you! I like the suit you chose, very cute.'

Ashrial giggled.

'Shall we get started then? We're going to need the whole night... and probably into tomorrow for that matter,' AQ telepathed to Ashrial.

'Yes. Let's begin by removing the human sphere and memories. We will archive them, allowing for reference only. Then we will change out connectors and bring in a new energetic spinal column, getting ready for the light being merge,' replied Ashrial.

Gee, it was weird hearing my newborn baby talking this way. I was used to babies that acted like babies, you know crying, eating, sleeping. This guy facilitates light being merges and archives!

* * *

In the morning, I opened my eyes to see Ashrial floating above me.

'Good morning,' he telepathed. 'There is a bit more work to do, but we need you to eat and walk around a bit first.'

My head still fuzzy, I replied: "Okay." Then tried to get up. I practically fell over in the process.

'You need to move slower, we've removed most of your ability to function normally,' telepathed Ashrial.

"Oh good," I replied, sarcastically. "That should make it easier to get around."

'Don't worry, the attitude is a side effect,' replied Ashrial, then flew off out the window, leaving me to figure out how to get up.

* * *

After eating, I lumbered back upstairs to lie down, barely making it to the bed.

"Roo, help," I called to her.

She popped over, helping me then tucking me in.

"Poor little mergy baby, you'll be okay soon. I promise," she said giving me a kiss and curling up next to me. Having her energy there with me seemed to make the process easier, less painful.

She sang quietly in my ear and I drifted into dream space.

In my dreams there were beings without Earth bodies all around me. They were flying and each one flitted over and touched me. It felt like they were giving me something, though I saw nothing. Then I saw my human form kind of disappearing and my body got really light. Next thing I knew I was floating around in this transparent body, emitting light from the inside.

I woke up again. "Roo?" I called.

"I'm here, muffin," she replied.

"It feels like they are drilling in my spine," I said.

Just then, Ashrial popped back in the room. 'We are finishing the new spinal column installation,' he transmitted. 'You will be done soon.'

I drifted back into dreams.

Chapter 10
Catalyst For The World

A few weeks later when things had settled a bit, like my light being merge, we called our group together again. My visions were better than ever!

Ashrial had been working with me to align me to my purpose as I left the old ways behind. Now it was time to create more room on the planet for everyone else that was ready or would be ready some day.

The Earth had gotten so disconnected from her people. We didn't respect her anymore. We wanted more buildings, more highways, more signs to direct us, more fences to keep us out. The Earth wanted to be free. She wanted to feel alive and she wanted those who resided on her and around her to feel free and alive, too.

Ashrial told me of the plan. To bring people together, heal the Earth and create more space for others. Together, our group would travel to places unknown and heal. Today was the beginning of that adventure. Our group was meeting up here at the house and Ashrial would take it from there!

* * *

Gartanimo approached me. "Mon, where we are going, it feels big," he said with a smile. "I like it!" He grabbed me to give me a hug, then growled into the air.

I had to admit, the energy was higher and going higher still. It made one feel the Earth, the sky and the animals.

I let out a growl, too.

Soni showed up with his crew, then others came. People walked in from the woods, from the driveway, animals flew in and ran on the ground, fairies, pixies, gnomes, elves, salamanders all showed up, creating a circle. She had called them all here, Mother Earth, and they heard her call.

As we stood in a circle the pixies sprinkled magical dust over us and with one blink of little Ashrial's eyes we were gone!

* * *

When we popped back up, our group was by the ocean. There were high cliffs around it and gorgeous beaches below. The sun was shining bright in the sky, the smell of salt filled my inhalation.

"She's calling us over here," I said to the group, leading them toward the water. We popped down the stairs.

The dogs seemed to get there first no matter which mode others used for travel. I think it is their natural instinct to run by the waves.

We all gathered in a circle, calling in energy from above us. Then like lightning, streaks of energy shot out all around us. I heard Gartanimo growl again.

I let out a howl, deep and long into the wind.

* * *

Within minutes we were playing music and dancing to heal the Earth. The animals were drawing in people from everywhere, the pixies were dancing with the salamanders, the earth was shaking from the sudden boost.

I watched as an energy grid covered the ground. The pattern in this part of the Earth had shifted, becoming matched with the healing light we brought.

I looked up to see more than a hundred people gathered, dancing, howling, holding hands.

They heard her call, Mother Earth, and they joined in the healing of their spirits.

* * *

In a flash we were gone again, leaving behind us a trail of possibility and unity.

Next we popped up in a deserted area of the Earth. Our group was growing. Some of the people and creatures from the beach came with us. It was beautiful to see it happen, this healing.

Gartanimo got out the didgeridoos, he had an unlimited amount of them, whoever wanted to play he had a didj for them. "Magic," he said with a laugh.

Dogs howled, pixies toned high-pitched notes, and other animals hit their tails against the ground or on drums and didjes moaned into the earth.

The ground began rumbling underneath us and rain came. This part of the Earth that almost never felt the cleansing of a good rain was now under it. A wet powerful rain, sounds of thunder filled the sky.

In a moment we popped from there, on to our next adventure.

* * *

The healing at this place looked overwhelming to some. We popped up in the middle of the city. Buildings like skyscrapers touched the clouds. The ground was covered in cement and tar. Metal walls of disconnection drove around on four wheels. And the people looked sad, all in a rush to get somewhere other than where they were.

We began singing and playing drums and cymbals.

Slowly people came to look or to tap their feet to the music. Ashrial blinked and made a beautiful grassy area with trees emerge right there where we stood! The pixies and fairies sprinkled magical dust and the animals opened their hearts wide to draw in the people and wake them from their sleep.

The rain came sprinkling over everything. Instead of leaving, the people stayed and then more joined them. We kept singing: "Remember who you are, remember who you are..."

Pretty soon they were laughing, even playing the drums. They left their metal vehicles behind to embrace this moment in connection with the Earth. She had called them, Mother Earth, and they heard her call.

Chapter 11

Cherish The Moment

Back at the house about a week later, construction of the center was beginning. The yard was always full of people working together to create. Sometimes creating a building, sometimes creating song.

Roo and I were spending time with Ashrial, learning more about his purpose and his vision for the Earth. The news of our center was spreading, people were calling to find out how to join in, animals were showing up wanting to stay.

One day as we sat on the grass talking, a cow moseyed over near us and began chewing the lawn. I telepathed: 'Good afternoon. How did you get here?'

It replied: 'I'm Bessie. Thanks for the grass.'

Roo and I started giggling. "They're coming from everywhere!" I yelled. "I love it!"

* * *

Soni, Raji and Eila were living in a yurt on the property. Their house sale was complete and they were getting back in touch with the earth. They wanted to feel more alive, so they slept upon the ground at night, stars overhead.

Eila didn't sleep much, her energy was out of sight lately. Her and Ashrial 'played' at nighttime. Actually, I think they were flying around the world, altering reality.... either way.

* * *

Gartanimo was leading the construction. He made sure everything they did matched what the Earth wanted. Which meant no wasting material or land and definitely no cutting down of trees. The center was being built up off the ground and built around the trees. Sireal was a big help for this part, he was very in tune with nature. He turned into Gartanimo's right hand gnome.

* * *

I was feeling peaceful inside, my purpose was composing experience around me. A thought was creation, a step was a blink and the answers were already known.

Roo and I were thinking about having another child. A light being from another planetary system had been sharing with us and was considering being born.

Life is good, I thought to myself. Just then, Roo gave me a kiss, causing my pockets to turn inside out and my hair to stand on end.

Chapter 12
My Dreams Must Have Been Big

Over the next month, I watched as it all unfolded. The center was nearly built and we were beginning the construction of a few cabins in the woods. We already had about twenty yurts set up at different spots on the land and in the forest.

There were now community gardens and a fruit orchard. The land had somehow grown a lot bigger.

Springs and creeks were popping up all over the place and people were coming here ready for healing. They were leaving their old ways behind and accepting more of themselves.

Roo, Ashrial and I helped with the landings. Meaning we helped their higher self land into the Earth body. I was surprised how many people were ready!

* * *

Our group continued to make trips around the world. We popped to numerous places to heal the Earth and her people. And the Earth was really waking up.

I noticed that people were building less and getting back in touch with their roots, in touch with the ground again. If they did build they were creating consciously in unison with the Earth.

* * *

Animals and otherworldly beings were part of everything we did. The earth, the rocks, the crystals, the plants, they all became part of the creation, sharing opinions and insights along with the rest. No one thought strange of it. It became natural, as it should be.

And the animals were really waking up! They were so purposeful. They wouldn't let you get away with anything. If you were trying to avoid something, they would put it right there in your face. You'd have to look at it then.

More and more pixies were coming out of hiding. Everyday folks were seeing them on flowers and in trees.

* * *

Since I landed my higher self into my body, I felt more serene. My heart remained open and I was always connected higher up, light ran through me and I wasn't scared anymore. The reality around me adjusted itself to my presence. I created this way. I created with others. I am like one petal on a flower. It takes others to create a full flower and to help it grow.

That's what we are creating here with the center and beyond.

That's what I call the Enlightened Way.